The longest Furrow Volume 2

First Published November 2010
© Fred Waterfall Publications (Countryman) 18.08.2013
mail@fcwaterfall.co.uk

Fred Watson

All money raised from the sale of these books goes to
Headways North Staffs.
The head injuries' charity

Chapter

Chapter 1

This was drawn by the Standard Fordson

One foot was still in a loop of rope. I remember as a kid of six or seven how we loved to have a ride on the empty trailers back to the field to be loaded.

On this occasion I had just missed my chance for a ride and I was on my own, when I though I would run and catch up and climb onto the back end of the wagon.

This was drawn by the Standard Fordson driven by my father, and with the noise of the engine I could not get his attention.

When carting the shoffs of corn (wheat) it had got to be roped on as it had got to travel across five fields and gateways, and the ropes were always wrapped up, drawn together in large loops and bound round the top with the last bit and hung under the back of each trailer.

When I caught up with the outfit, I thought I could put my foot in the swinging rope and claw myself up the backend of the gormers and onto the trailer. But it did not turn out like that at all, having slipped with my grip I fell backwards to the ground, it was only a few inches off the ground, but fell.

Trouble was one foot was still in a loop of rope and it started dragging me across the fields and the old Fordson could only go at eight miles per hour (thank goodness). I rolled this way and that, I curled up to try and free me foot time and again with no luck. Eventually one of dads helpers saw my dilemma and stopped him, all he did was to unhook my foot, put me across his knee and gave me four of five good smacks across my back side to teach me a lesson, across a back side that was already battered and bruised from the drag, it was one lesson well learned.

I Remember Father bought a tractor

Father bought a tractor,
To help the horses out,
Twas a green Standard Fordson,
Bit noisy had to shout,
Spade lug wheels iron up front,
To give it grip in mud,
War time demanded ,plough up grass,
To grow lot more spud.

Winter ploughing with a tractor,
Quicker it would be,
But colder with the sitting,
And no walking so you see,
You cannot have it both ways,
To hurry was a must,
So on with army great coat,
A hat and scarf, no dust.

We came to move to Seighford,
To spade lugs he fitted bands,
To stop the lumpy driving,
From Doxey, need many hands,
Lot of road work at the Beeches,
Up to furthest fields,
Rubber tyres then were fitted,
With the higher yields,

As the years went by,
We lads we kept on growing,
We learned to drive the tractor,
As trailers men were loading

7

it progressed on to bindering,
To cut the corn make sheaves,
The men were all occupied,
To stook the corn till eve.

The tractor getting worn and old,
Its steering getting stiff,
On every blooming corner,
Became a bigger loop and if
Only it would straighten up,
And not run corn down,
Father on the binder would be
Warring his worst frown.

His anger at a driving era,
Was there for all to see,
If the whip he had for horses,
It would soon be used on me,
It soon became apparent, that,
Good driving is a must,
At each and every corner,
The steering to adjust.

———————

As we progressively older and into our lower teens, we in turn were able to start driving the old Fordson, the first most important job that seemed to go on for a week or so none stop was that of bindering the corn, that was where we took it in turns to drive. (Corn - wheat ,oats and barley and sometimes beans and often had a field of dredge corn,) which consisted of barley, oats, wheat, peas and beans, this was a difficult crop to binder as if you did it too early the wheat would be still green, if you did it too late the barley or oats would be shedding. When the dredge corn was threshed the grain was in them days as near to a balanced ration for the cattle as you could get all home grown.

During the war and for quite a few years after imported grains, maize and soya were in short supply as were groundnut, palm colonel, and linseed cake. These were the by product of the oil crushing mills in Liverpool where Bibby's produced a balanced cow corn in cubes, or was it their soap factory (remember ASTRA perfumed soap, it made a change from the war time carbolic soap) where they utilized by-product into dairy cake.

It was on a factory visit to the docks (Father had started using Bibby's Dairy cubes) at Liverpool to Bibby's factory that they also took you round the soap factory as well, and they even gave out a few paper wrapped bars of their Astra soap to each of their visitors, I can't tell you how thrilled mother was with "her" perfumed soap, but needless to say we never got a smell of it.

At the docks we saw no end of pair of shire horses pulling wooden wheeled wagons about with up to six tons at a time, of coarse it was all level pulling on cobbled and paved streets in and around the docks from ships to warehouses, but of coarse Bibby's factory was right on the dock side.

Another thing we saw that day was steam Lorries or wagons still working from docks to warehouses a bit further inland, in fact when we were going home on the coach we saw then them chuffing along the main roads at amazing speeds fully loaded.

I seem to have got side traced from my original story; the old Fordson was getting well worn by the time we got to working it, in particular the steering. On full lock the inside front wheel would turn its angle almost to touch the engine, and it took an enormous effort to get it from there to the other lock. On cutting corn with the binder this happened on every corner, and occasionally did not make it soon enough, and ran some of the corn down in the process.

Father always rode "shot gun" on the binder as he was very particular as to how low the straw was cut, he almost licked it off the ground, and he adjusted the string to where the shoffs were tied according to the length of straw, and originally would have had to steer the three shire horses pulling it as well.

But now we were steering the coarse, and any deviation would be shouted at of very severely and heavily frowned at, in fact we were glad that he did not still have the long whip in its holder that he could "title" the shires with or I've no doubt it would have soon been used on us. Needless to say our arms got stronger by the minuet and rarely ran into, or even edged the crop again.

We got that used to the job it was up to us to convert the binder back onto its road wheels, on to the next field and back into cutting mode again, we were doing it "Formula One" stile pit stops, a lot faster than the men could do it so they let us get on with it.

Father always had a policy "Flog the young" but then another saying he had contradicted that "Wear the old buggers out fust"

Chapter 2

The Joys of running a Rest Home

About twenty years ago, my misses was keen to earn a bit of money running her own business. She was very good, nay I must say excellent with old people, and there seemed to be a niche for country people wanting accommodation in rest homes but not wanting to go into a built up areas of the town. So without any formal training we set about converting three rooms of our house into an "old people's rest home".

With no advertising we had our first old lady Anne, who had suffered a stroke and was not safe to live on her own. As it turned out Anne lasted the whole time that we run this rest home, (fifteen years) she was the first and was also the last, and received her letter from the QUEEN and went on to be one hundred and one. Really it was a sad end for her as she slipped off her chair one evening and broke the main bone in her leg half way up her shin, from which she did not last long in hospital, . In the fifteen years we have had three gentle men and eight ladies who had enjoyed their last years of their lives with us.

One of the exceptional characters we had was John, John had farmed all his life and was in his element tutoring me on how to run the farm. He had been a resident at a big nursing home in town and kept "running away" just to be able to see some fields.

They had to send staff out in their cars looking for him almost every day. He was a man who milked cows and got up early all his life, and was up and away and off outside before breakfast, often lunch time before he was found.

John's daughter was at her whit's end with worry, as they had started to ring her to come looking for her dad.

Then she heard of what we were doing at Yews Farm, and came to suss us out, but of course with only three residents,

11

we were full. So we were asked if she could send her dad John when we had a vacancy.

Eventually John came as a resident on the farm, he liked to count and keep an eye on the cattle just down the road, and they were suckler cows getting close to calving. He would tidy up the troughs along the bull beef sheds. And every morning he loaded up a wheel barrow with timber so full I could only just push it, this was for my log / straw burning boiler that heated the house.

However this wore him out by lunch time and he rested all afternoon, but he was as happy as a dog with two tails. At Mid morning at ten thirty we always have a coffee break, but John was always too dam busy to stop work, so his coffee was taken out to him. The ruck of timber that he worked at was by the end of an old cowshed, and in the end of this shed we put an old arm chair, this tempted him to sit down to have his coffee, after all he was in his eighties, sometimes he fell asleep then had to rouse him for lunch much to his embarrassment of sleeping on the job.

John took his jobs seriously and would start promptly at nine am, but this one day he realized there were some rats lodging in his wood ruck, so came across the yard to fetch Matt, my son, with his ferrets, Matt and john put the most reliable ferret down to find its way through the wood pile, and they could see a some rats moving about so they got a stick apiece and started prodding into the pile, shouting with excitement every time one was spotted , but I think John must have prodded the ferret by mistake as the ferret jumped out of the wood and bit John on the ankle, this did not deter old John he was well used to bumps and bangs through his life.

But what he had not bargained for was the he was on tablets that thinned his blood, and when he bled it would not clot as normal. So half an hour later, when they came in for lunch John's boot was literally full of blood.

Of coarse my misses who is responsible for him thought he

had lost his foot, then pulled the blood soaked boot and sock off and washed his foot, then could then see it was just a small bite, then applied some antiseptic and a plaster, but John had lost a lot of blood and was pale. Matt and I and John were told off about recklessly hunting rats with ferrets, particularly with a very elderly gentle man who was very unsteady on his feet. It must have brought back happy memories for John as after that we laughed many times about his ratting escapade, and it was only later that his daughter found out, but by then even she could see the funny side.

On another occasion the local hunt was to meet on the village green right outside our front wicket, John in his lifetime had always been a keen follower of the hunt so was keen to go onto the green to see the meet. There were many folk he new and all came talking to him, we took him a seat and his morning coffee out, and then after a short while the hunt moved off to draw the first covert. When the girls helping went out to fetch him in again, John was missing, we thought at first he must have gone with the other hunt followers who were on foot up into St Chads church yard, where they always went where there was a grand stand view of the hounds in full cry when they drew the first wood. Matt and I went to look in the church yard when all the spectators were getting into their cars, but no one had seen John, we went all round the grave stones thinking he may have fell down, because we knew he could not get up again An hour had gone by and his lunch was ready and the misses was getting extremely worried for his safety, and after another half hour she rang his daughter. There were three of us searching all round the farm and the village, and even further afield in a cars but still he could not be found.

Much later in the afternoon a car drew into our yard, and out stepped John, it was only his old mate Tom (in his eighties) from years ago, had seen him, and John had got into his car without telling anyone, they had had a good three hours of following the hunt.

When ask was he hungry, he said he had some of Tom's and a drink from his flask. It was a relief that he was okay and not hurt in any way.

Now being so active in his mind John hankered for a four wheel scooter battery powered so he could get out and about under his own steam, this was all right but when we realized where he wanted to go, some of it was along a main road with no pavements, the thought of him in his buggy going at five miles per hour, and traffic passing him at over fifty miles per hour that was not on. His intention was to visit his daughter some seven miles away, this was what he had done when he drove his car every week but they had to stop him from driving for his own safety, so John did not get his scooter.

In the garden we had a couple of rows of strawberries, and John I remember from years ago on his farm had a very tidy and productive garden, so John decided he would weed among the strawberries for us with a hoe. He was watched carefully from the kitchen window to see he was okay, and then at the next moment he was in the rows on his hands and knees. This went on for nearly the next hour, then it was realized that he had fell down, and while he was down he just kept on weeding.

He was very independent, and did not like asking for help from a woman, even to be helped back onto his feet, so he just kept busy.

John told us tales of his first small farm called Spurly Brook, where he and his wife milked cows by hand with the cowshed directly connected to the house,

He was able to step out of his kitchen into the cowshed, but unfortunately the cowshed was at the top side of the house, so the urine dropped by the cows drained in an open gully through the house kitchen. This must have been very basic living and in the 1920's. Bet he kept that gully well washed out.

It was a very sad day when John had to go for an operation on his throat, it got that he could not swallow solid food. It was arranged that his daughter would pick him up at 11am, so John went out do his normal chores - fill the wheel barrow full of timber for me to take to the boiler house, then in again to get changed ready for his hospital appointment.

We weren't to know that that was the last time we should see John, as the operation was a very risky one that he never recovered from. He was a hard working and cheerful man all his life and for him to load that wheel barrow before he went into hospital meant he had work every day of his life, right to his last day at our home.

It was an absolute privilege for us to have had such a gentleman, who would talk all about his life and be our adviser in many ways other than farming as well.

Hears to the memory of John Ecclestone he would have loved to have read this one about gardening.

Happiness is nothing more than good health and a bad memory.
Albert Schweitzer (1875-1965)

Chapter 3

To Cut and Cart the Kale Blog (Mid 1940's)

In winter time father grew Kale, to be used up to the turn of the year, after that the cows went onto mangels that were kept safe in a covered hog to protect them from the frost.

The kale was Marrow Stem and drilled early April it would grow up to six foot high, as the name suggests over half the feed was in the centre of the stem, the marrow.

This was cut by hand and loaded in the afternoon by the cowman onto a flat four wheeled dray pulled by one of fathers shire horses. It was then thrown out onto a grass field near to the sheds for the cows to go out for exercise the following morning and brows their ration of kale.

Cows in them days were all tied in stalls and only went out once a day in winter, so the sheds could be cleaned out and bedded up properly.

Some days we would go with the cowman Philip, he was only a young chap in his twenties, and a bit of a reckless driver (of the horse), like turning the horse and the front turntable of the dray quarter turn and the horse would snatch to get the load moving, on this one occasion tipping the load onto its side.

That would not have been too disastrous only my brother and I were buried under the load. I believe Philip had a tremendous scramble to get us out, I know I was first out and standing by on my own in a daze, and after a short while my brother emerged all muddy an shaken.

On the way home we were sworn to secrecy on what had happed not to tell our father (the old chap as Philip called him) or he might have got cussed in no uncertain terms. The secret was kept and Philip kept his job for another twenty years.

To Cut and Cart the Kale

We used to go with cowman Philip,
To cut and put out the kale,
This was done with horse and flat dray,
Come sun or snow or hail,
Half and hour to chop the stems,
And fell them in a row,
Then load them up, stems to the middle,
Cold its' down to zero.

Old Flower she turns and pulls hard,
As she goes to the gate,
Through muddy ruts we had to walk,
For a ride we had to wait,
We were not very big and had to be lifted,
Up on top of the load,
Down hill now all the way home,
A half a mile on the road.

Into the turf close to the farm,
Throw the stems off in the field,
Cows to eat the following day,
And hope to improve their yield,
Winter feeding of the dairy herd,
A never ending job,
Nice to get into warm cowsheds,
Cows in their bedding flop.

On this one day when we were with him,
Loading up the kale,
Turned old Flower, tipped the load,
Such a sorry tale,

Slid the load of Kale off,
All over me and my brother,
Philip dug fast to find us,
As under the load we'd smother,

We were OK a little dazed,
Soon came round and recovered,
Squared the horse and wagon,
To load up again we staggered,
On the way home Philip asked us,
Not to tell the old chap,
Father never knew why,
We were covered in mud in a mishap.

On the way up to the kale field with Philip he stopped (he may have stopped before when he was on his own) under an overhanging nut bush, he pulled old Dolly the shire well over onto the grass verge and well up under the hedge and stopped well under the thick of a good crop of hazel nuts.

He had the long cutting hook that he cut the kale with, and pulled down those nuts that would otherwise be out of reach, we were already standing on the wagon. As kids this was exiting as we filled our pockets and Philip cracked some for us to eat. Then a loud voice came from the big house across the grassy orchard, "oooyyyy what are you up to", they had seen the bushes swaying about and came out to investigate. We all went flat on the wagon and flapped the reigns on old Dolly's back and we were off. They knew who it was and what we were up to, and as no damage had been done nothing was ever said. But they never realised how many nuts we had got.

I Remember Philip Boulton.

At the Beeches we had a cowman,
His name was Philip Boulton,
He liked his beer at weekend,
Was at the pub quite often,
Lived in a cottage by the shop,
Front door opened from the pavement,
It had low doors and ceilings,
And dormer window casements.

Only a young chap just got married,
And never learned to drive,
Went everywhere on his bike,
Except the pub till he'd revive,
The bike it had low handle bars,
And a dynamo driven headlight,
A sad a crumpled saddle bag,
Nothing in it to excite.

He always wore a bib and
Brace overall, And a singlet vest,
Even in the winter time,
When working bared his chest,
Wellingtons or wellies,
With turned down tops so short,
Even in the summer time,
No working boots to sport.

A round faced man,
Hair combed flat back,
Receding over each temple,
And he never wore a hat,

What few teeth he had,
Dentist ventualy pulled the lot,
And a full set of dentures fitted,
No more for him the rot.

He looked after all the cows,
Fed and milked them all,
In the winter had some help,
Cleaning out the stalls,

Often us lads would carry milk,
To the dairy there to cool
Filling up the churns for transport,
Before and after school.

He'd harness up the horse,
On afternoons in winter,
Cut and load kale onto the wagon,
He was quite a sprinter,
Throw it out around the field,
Next day for the cows,
They're turned out for exercise,
And the kale to browse.

For many years he stayed with us,
Until he saw more money,
A factory job and no weekend,
He left in such a hurry,
His cottage was never used again,
Pulled down to pile of rubble,
Bungalow built on the site,
Back off the pavement out of trouble

Being a drinking man he frequented the Holly Bush pub two or three evenings a week only just up the road. When, as kids we occasionally called at his cottage, we would be offered a cup of tea, but not cups as we were used to, these were pint sized, he had nothing smaller.

There was a little cast iron stove with the huge kettle boiling hanging from a hook on the chimney crane, his toasting fork that he or his wife would poke or re-arrange the logs on the fire, and a square table in the middle of the small room covered with a colourful piece of worn oilcloth. Each side of the fire was what passed for arm two chairs, any one else had to sit on the old wooden kitchen chairs. In front of the fire for the kids to sit on was the peg rug made out of strips of cloth from worm out clothing.

I think the house had been built before the roadside pavement had been established because from his front door you stepped down a step into the house, the door opened directly onto the pavement.

The doors could not have been much more than five foot six and inside the beams in the living room come kitchen no more the six foot.

I suppose in them day's people were not so tall, or maybe it was the estate thought they would save bricks by only building a cottage with very low rooms

As I remember it , it was the only cottage that had round edge tiles on the roof, quite fancy for a farm cottage, and what's the betting that the tiles had come off another larger house that had perhaps been demolished. Who knows?

Remember, people will judge you by your actions, not your intentions. You may have a heart of gold – but so does a hard boiled egg.
<u>Unknown</u>

Chapter 4

A Hay Sweep Fitted to the Standard Fordson

Fire was always a major hazard near the railway lines, a cinder blown out of the chimney with the smoke of the old steam engines, would land in a bit of dry grass and catch fire; this would burn with a bit of following wind up the embankment quite often burning the fence on the way.

Father had a field of wheat ready for the binder, but before he got to it the wind had blown fire through the fence into twelve acre standing crop, and nothing anyone could do to stop it once it got hold.

On another occasion it was a field of hay that he and the men had been working in all day, and were aiming to collect it after evening milking. This was done with a hay sweep fitted on the front of fathers Standard Fordson, the crop being pushed up to a stack in the middle of the field.

But when we went to the field it was just black smouldering stubble, it had all burnt except in a couple of corners, the half stack of hay left over from the previous year had gone as well.

The lengths men who worked along the railway line, try to keep the embankments cut, and burnt off in a controlled way, but sometimes a cinder would do it for them when no one was about.

The railway "lengths men" were a gang of about six men who maintained the railway tracks and fences on their length between half way to Stafford and half way to Norton Bridge based at Great Bridgeford. Father got to know them well as they were also in the home guard.

It was these same lengths men who would hop over the railway fence when father was cutting large field of corn for half an hour and help stook the corn, with a gang like that it soon got done.

It was the same again when it came to loading the farm wagons with shoffs of corn, father would make sure he took down plenty of pitch forks as there was five or six in the gang.

The cart was loaded in about five minuets flat, and off back to the farm with his load drawn behind his Standard Fordson, and back with the next one in half an hour.

No money seemed to change hands, but eggs, taters, and other produce on ration was exchanged for work done, and in the case of the engine driver he got half a pig.

The main meeting for these exchanges was the home guard meeting at the Village hall.

The Home Guard Contraband

The railway line it ran through,
Some of father's land,
He got to know the railway men,
Quite a happy band,
They were in the home guard
And all the farm men too,
They often jumped over the fence,
To load a wagon or two.

For this he gave them taters,
Or anything they hadn't got,
Often at the home guard meetings,
The sergeant got forgot,
For this is where it all changed hands,
Just behind his back,
If they ever got found out,
They'd be on the rack.

An engine driver was among them,
He'd got what we want,
He slowed his train by the field,
Tender full of coal he flaunt,
Every morning at nine thirty,
Rolled off big lumps of coal,
Father loaded it on his cart,
This man he did extol.

A coal house full of best steam coal,
Mother to do the cookin,
Big bright fire that roared round flue,
She was so pleased herein,
Only cost a half a pig,
Its contraband you see,
Delivered by dad and Eric in a coffin,
The law could not foresee.

———————

Most of the tea coupons are used and the cheese and fats and sugar coupons. There no meat coupons left, but mother took all the books with her and tended to use all the coupons out of one book before she picked up the next, but then you should not use coupons in advance of the date.

So she must have saved up and got a "stock" of coupons in the various books. This book is for the year May 1953 through to May 1954 but then some time early in that period rationing must have been withdrawn and rationing ended.

There is twenty six pages in the book and on the front has a F.O. CODE No. M – J – 1 and a serial no. AT 565118 Ministry of Food and my name and address.

We had our own eggs and milk, and early on in the war mother would make cheese and butter, and very occasionally she would make some bread.

Now Eric had a Big Car

I remember during the war,
And after for a while,
Everyone had ration books,
Cues could stretched a mile,
In the village it was not too
Bad, contraband it moved,
Under the policeman's nose,
The law they disapproved.

Now Eric had a big car,
With a carrier on the back,
And when someone died,
The coffin he'd take on rack,
Covered in a black cloth,
Everyone knew what it was,
From the wheelwrights' shop,
No attention draws.

The coffin it was just made,
No lining did it have,
Father had just killed a pig,
Exchange for coal he halved,
Laid the half pig in the coffin,
For transport to his mate,
Then lined the coffin and delivered,
Just a little late.

———————————

The village wheelwright made the coffins and dug the graves
and laid people out when they died.

This is a picture of Eric crossing the pool opposite Seighford Hall with his shire horses going out to the fields.

Education is not the filling of a pail, but the lighting of the fire.
W. B. Yeats.

Chapter 5

Farm safety a Topic on most peoples minds

A Topic for as long as I can remember.

Over the years I have had upwards of fifteen school leavers, some starting while still at school, but every one without exception had some sort of bump or miner accident on the way.

I recall one who was loading strawy box muck by hand with me, before we had fore end loaders. To get a bigger load this lad jumped on the top to level out the load way above the trailer side boards, but just above him was a pair of electric wires, very old and with ragged insulation.

He stood up and caught the back of his head on the wires and he dropped like a stone right into the pile of muck we were loading. He was okay but wondered what had hit him, and it turned out to be one of many near misses that this lad was to have. After a number of road crashes he got killed at the age of twenty two, by just shear speed.

Way back in my twenties I recall taking a Friesian bull up the lane about half a mile, he was always all right to lead in the yard , but as we got nearer to the field of heifers in the distance he started to bounce, and picked up speed and I still clung onto him.

Then being along side of his shoulder I was getting pushed toward a steep hedge bank, on top of the hedge bank was a three foot hawthorn hedge, some eight foot in all.

Next thing I knew I was standing the other side of that hedge still hanging on to the long chain that I was leading him by.

Basically I had run along side of the bank gradually being pushed higher up it, and with the speed I had thankfully cleared the hedge on top. I have used that lane all the years

since and can never come to terms of how I cleared that height, but when you are in a tight spot, its surprising what you are capable of.
Fortunately I was not on the end of his horns.

One of the most dangerous things that lads tended to do is to hitch a tow chain to the top link point on the tractor. In the days I am talking about there were no cabs or roll bars, so a rearing tractor would turn over backward flat onto the driver in the spilt of a second. I made a point of never leaving the top link pin in place and not send any lad out with a chain.

Another lad had a narrow escape when he was out with the rota spreader, he drove the wrong way round the field, in other words he drove on the slurry that had been spread from the previous load, and on going up a slight gradient and along side of the slope as well.
The spreader started to swing sideways directly towards a steep drop, the tractor start wheel slip and also hung back in the same direction, then the whole outfit was sliding backward and gathering speed.
This I witnessed with my own eyes from the distance, and saw it all disappear down the steep drop, the whole thing stayed in line and as it came to a stop the front of the tractor whipped round into a jack-knife.
No damage was done, the lad hung onto the steering wheel and stayed in the seat.
It was one of those thing that you can see from the distance, and could predict what was going to happen, but could do dam all about it.

As a lad myself on that same slope a gang of us were loading loose hay onto a four wheel dray towing a hay loader behind it (A Pitcher).

This was before we had a baler and before contractor balers were about, we were just going down this same slope, when the pitcher blocked. Two men were on the load and I (the lad) was driving the tractor, so I stopped and got off to help unblock the blockage.

Both men jumped down off the near full load and decided that the pitcher had got to be tilted forwards onto its nose. One man went under the back of the dray on his knees and pulled the hitch pin, it was a bit tight but he managed, only to realise that the load and the tractor was moving away from him.

Nothing was said but he thought I was on the tractor until he looked and saw me behind the pitcher helping to unblock it. NO ONE was on the tractor.

By this time it was nearly up to running speed and heading for this steep slope, fortunately the one chap had a good turn of speed and mounted the drawbar and reached forwards and turned the steering wheel across the slope and it all came to a stop.

The tractor did have a parking brake but it had not been applied, the pitcher mechanism was wheel driven and being blocked held the outfit when we stopped. Moral of this story is to always apply the parking brake every time you get off.

Another example, one about my grand daughter and the ride on lawn mower a few years ago. At the age of twelve she was getting very keen to learn to drive and the only thing I would let her drive then was the lawn mower.

Set her going, showing he the gears the clutch and throttle. After ten minuets it was only top gear and only full throttle. This went on for quite a few weekends until one afternoon she came walking /limping back to the house.

On investigation she had mistook the turning circle of the mower and still going at full throttle had rammed at full speed (about seven miles per hour) under the back of a parked grain trailer.

The mower is one of those with a racy sloping tapered front so wedge very tight under the back cross member. She had slid up the seat and bumped her knees and the steering wheel had gone into her tummy. The mower was recovered with a scratched bonnet, and the grand daughter had a very severely dented pride, and bruised knees. It was a thing she will always remember and a good lesson learned without too much grief.

I won't let her drive the old tractors, the ones with no cab and no roll bar, she now has learned to drive the Agrotron and is very happy about that as it has a good radio and tape player.

Its still got its doors and still got all its windows, the foot pedals are light and easy for her to use, the seat and the steering wheel both adjust, and now got used where all the gears are, and four wheel drive is just a rocker switch.

The only thing I cannot get her to learn is when turning (chain harrowing) at the end of the field, on short ground turn away from the ditch and circle into the field. Turning towards the ditch you have got to judge your turning circle very accurately or you will soon be in the ditch.

This following one is about my workshop, and the pile of tools that are thrown on the bench some of which missed, a bit of clear floor space to walk up the middle. The off cuts and other items deemed to be too good to throw away are saved and left where they land. Only I know where everything is, it's just a matter of finding it.

Axle Stand and his Mate Jack

Axle Stand and his mate, Hydraulic Jack,
Live in the workshop, right at the back,
When they're called out together they work,
Lifting things heavy, they call it teamwork.

Adjustable Spanner, he lives hanging on nail,
Expected to fit every nut, in the box he assail,
He's first responder, carried into the field
No hammer to hand, a thraping to weald.

Poor old Hack he loses teeth from his blade,
Abused and used cut anything for what he's not made,
Hack Saw gets hacked off, thrown on the bench,
Landing on top of him, a great heavy old wrench

32

Open and Ring Spanner, Siamese twins in the tools,
Kept in a rolled bag, with pocket like modules,
Twenty of them, all different sizes,
Clean and in line should win all the prizes.

Pillar the drill, stands aloof in the corner,
His own leg to the floor, and quite a loner,
His energy comes down, a wire from the switch,
Grips bit in his chuck,turns quick without glitch.

Ball Pane is Hammer, comes in a good many sizes,
Large for the blacksmith, hot metal he teases
Small one that the Mrs. keep's, in the cupboard draw,
And ones in between, working all have loud guffaw.

Claw is another member, of the same clan,
Pull bent nails, blame the hammer and not man,
Soon break the stale, when pulled and abused,
Thrown onto the side, no stale and unused.

We know how it should be all tidy and straight,
But never got time to put back all polish it's late,
As long as I can walk up the middle OK,
And find where I chucked it, Neat pile to display.

**It is one of the worst errors to suppose that there is any
path for safety except that of duty**   William

Chapter 6

Fathers School Days

Father had been brought up by his uncle in the 1920`s, a single man who put him to work long hours before and after school. The school was a village in south Staffordshire a mile or so across fields and footpaths. Upon arriving at school the children's boots were inspected, inevitably on wet mornings they would muddy and no excuse would be aloud for not polishing your boots before setting out to school.
Hand Milking.
Milking was the first job every morning, (even on school mornings) the cows rounded up from the "night pasture" (usually the nearest couple of fields by the buildings), every cow knew her own stall, tied up and ready for milking. Out with the buckets and stools, turn your cap round and head under the easiest cow to milk. With two gallon in the bottom of the bucket, there would be as much again of froth protruding out of the cone shaped pail.
Some were restless and fidgety, some with tails down right filthy, some were just hard to milk, some had pendulous udders almost to the ground and the teats pointing east west (these were usually the heaviest yielder's but the most awkward to milk)
When the cows were all in milk it meant there was up to eight or ten cows each.
Milk was carried in pails to the dairy by the farm house, tipped through a cotton wool filter to take out all that might fall into it (straw?) and into a high D shape receiving tub.
 There was a brass tap on the front so that you could graduate the flow of milk down the ribbed cooling block, locally called a fridge, this was made of copper and plated with tin (or some white metal) the copper a good conductor of heat and the tin easy to clean.

34

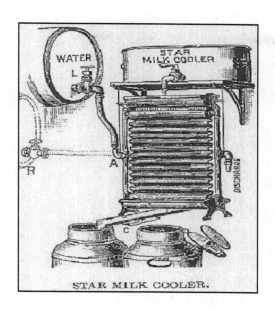

STAR MILK COOLER.

Water from the well is pumped and flowed up the inside of the fridge, the milk flowed down the outside, the aired water that left the fridge went into a cow trough for them to drink when they were turned out from the sheds.

From the fridge the milk dropped into the large seventeen gallon churns, all hell would be let loose if anyone let a churn run over, which it inevitably did from time to time, it was one of those things you only ever did once.

Next job was to harness the half legged Cob, put him in the shafts of the float, back up to the dairy, load the churns and tie them to keep them from slipping or moving.

The driver, usually the youngest lad (my father), about twelve or thirteen would be trusted to encourage the horse to move swiftly toward the station, but not too swiftly out of the yard gate as it was a forty five degree turn round the end of the roadside ditch, this taken at speed would "Spill the Milk".

On down the narrow single track road you would be fairly safe, as long as your Cob did not try to load himself up in the back of the neigh boughs float pulled by a slow and old "Hack" (and usually driven by one as well).

As you got near the station it was like the "Gold Rush" fortunately everyone going the same direction. Fittest and fastest horses at the front of the queue, (if they did the milking on time,) and wait for the train, when it did come the floats were backed up in turn to the rail wagon, the full ones duly labelled loaded, and the tomorrows empties taken home.

Then into the house, get changed and off to school with his boots polished and instant cane if he was late.

Fingers (or not)

In his school holidays father in his early teens would be sent off to mow with a pair of Shires. First the blade had to be sharpened like a razor in the barn, by his uncle, this made it easier for the horses to pull, and always take a spare one with you as well, half way through the morning the blade would go "dull" and block, so it needed to be changed.

It was during a blockage that the fingers of the mower had to be cleared, and to an inexperienced lad like my dad he lifted the blade from the lever by the seat, then walked round to the back of the blade, and cleared it with his hand, (not with a stick) he should have put the blade out of gear.

At an unfortunate moment one horse did little more than stamp his foot, the blade did a quick couple of zithers and father lost two of his fingers, his little finger was taken back to the first joint and the flap of skin stitched over to cover the hole, similarly the next finger was cut off above the second joint the same again, taken off at the next lower joint. Stitching back on was not an option in them days and you did your work with what you have left

36

I Remember Fathers Fingers

A tale he told us while working for his uncle Dan, he must have been around thirteen years old

Father lost two fingers,
While mowing hay one day,
He was helping Uncle Dan on the meadows,
Not at all at play,
Only thirteen started working,
Horses in the shaft,
The mower blocked with grass,
Clearing it by hand (how daft)

He lifted blade and went round back,
While it was still in gear,
One horse did stamp his foot at flies,
And gave the blade two shithers,
This was just enough no doubt,
Cut two fingers in one go,
He never said how he stopped,
The blood, there must have been a flow.

The little finger it was off,
Above the lower joint,
The next was off above second,
Clean cut to a point,
Hospital took one off at knuckle,
And stitch the flap of skin,
Tuther left half a stub,
Of finger what a sin.

No safety men to bother them,
It was get him back to work,
They healed so slow, it was a blow,
But not a time to shirk,
A motor bike he bought one day,
To get about much quicker,
It had a belt to drive, hand clutch,
And blow up tyre,

Mother he did find one day,
While he was out on bike,
He gave a lift and she did find,
How cold the bike could be,

Knit pair of gloves did she,
To fit his fingers short,
Then regularly did see her out,
And then began to court.

Round the table Sunday breakfast,
Father told us tales,
Of how he helped his uncle Dan,
Less fingers and no bales,
We had to always asked him,
To tell us that again,
Of how he lost his fingers,
And all about the pain.

Father with his shire horses Flower and Dolly some years later

When you point your finger at someone, three fingers are pointing back at you.
Anonymous

Chapter 7

The Bacon Rashers were 50/50 Fat and Lean

We watched all this when we were kids,
Fingers in our ears,
Then bang the butcher shot him,
And cut its throat mid tears,

Every house and cottage in the village had a pig sty, and the farms had three or four sties where they would keep an old sow and breed there own pigs needed for fattening. There would be only one boar in the area and most of the sows would be taken to visit him at the appropriate time.

The cottagers would buy a weaner and feed it mostly on scraps from the house and garden, nothing was ever wasted, if it was edible (for the pig) it was fed to it. Bear in mind that most had big families and a large cultivated garden, and all vegetables and fruit were grown and some would be preserved for winter use. Potatoes and carrots hogged, onions dried and strung up fruit bottled and apples trayed and stored and of coarse there was always a hen run for eggs and some for killing for the table.

Back to the pig, as it got fat, and I mean fat, not like the lean "baconer" types of today, you would start think about its slaughter, and where the village pig bench was, and clear a clean place for it to be killed. Also you would need to think about where to hang it up for it to "set" for five or six days.

On the pig killing day at home, the boiler would be filled and boiling ready, pig bench scrubbed off; the butcher would set out his equipment, including his pistol, and a noose that would be put over the pig's snout and behind the pig's fang top teeth.

Butcher did the leading and two more pushing from behind to encourage the pig out of the sty where it had resided almost all its life. Along side the pig bench the pig's legs were lifted from under it and rolled onto the bench then without any hesitation the butcher put the pistol to its head and shot it.

It was a struggle to keep it on the bench as its legs whipped and flailed, while the knife went into its throat. A bucket was on hand to catch the blood for the black pudding, and thing quietened down as the kicking stopped.

All the while this was going on us kids would be peeping round the corner as the squealing and noise and the gun going off we had our fingers in our ears, also the gushing of blood frightened us.

Then one at a time we went in closer to see the steaming pig being scraped after hot water was poured over it. Then saw the butcher dip the pigs feet in the scalding water as if to clean them only to realise in the back of his scraper was a big hook which he hooked into the pig's trotter and ripped the hoof off each of its toes.

Next they cut a slot in the pig's hocks and inserted a "tree", it's like a heavy wooden coat hanger that they will lift the pig up to the beam above.

As if he was drawing a line down the middle of the pig's belly, the butcher stroked his sharp knife gently down to reveal the pig's guts. As these gradually oozed out into a wheel barrow that was put in place for them to slide into. Useful things like the kidneys heart and liver were saved and hung up on a butchers hook. Inside there was what they called a vale, which was also saved, this was to wrap faggots and had a certain amount of fat in the webbing. Off with the trotters and the head, and then it was left to "set".

The cutting up came some days later the main quarters left whole to be salted down, some fresh pork was saved for immediate use, and some pork went to some friends who also killed a pig some months before.

The head was boiled and the meat and brains was compacted into big basins to make brawn and the jelly stock from the boiled trotters poured over to top the basins up level. When covered these would keep for a reasonable while, and tipped out then sliced and used as you would corned beef.

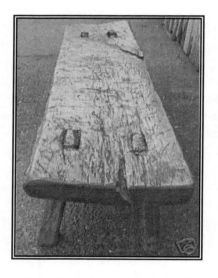

This is like the pig bench that went around the village

During the war time rationing you were supposed to get permission to kill a pig but I suspect a good many got them killed and distributed without anyone knowing.

The Cottage Pig Sty

Cottages had a pig sty, as most houses did,
Fatten up a piglet on scraps from house is fed,
Kept it eight or ten months, till it's good and fat,
Shame to see it come to its end, often had a chat.

Always had a name, knew when it's time for food,
For this it's always ready, door it often chewed,
Killed for pork and bacon, hams in salt well cured,
Hanging in the pantry, muslin covered till matured.

There is no power on earth that can neutralise the influence of a high, simple, and useful life.
Booker T. Washington (1856-1915)

Chapter 8

The old Seed Fiddle

He pushed and pulled the bow, with each stride he took,
For the seed must spread thinly, according to the book.

I still have a seed fiddle that I used to sow seed mixture in the corners of the fields for the stewardship schemes. I keep it in the office on top of a cabinet where it won't get damaged or run over by a tractor.

Father always had one for broadcasting grass seeds, but according to its instruction card pinned to it you can sow anything that will go through the aperture (that rules out potatoes). It also tells you how to calibrate and set the regulating lever.

If you have an Aero seed fiddle the chances are that the instructions are un readable or even worn away or just got torn off. However here is a copy of the exact instructions that should be followed

THE "AERO" BROARDCASTER
HAND SEED SOWER

WORKING DIRECTIONS

Place the stick of bow in position, by putting it through the coiled spring immediately in rear of distributor bobbin; fix end on stick; give thong one turn round bobbin the pass it through hole in handle of bow and secure tightly.

To alter machine to sow different quantities per acre, loosen the winged nut on bottom of box, set lever to number required, then tighten winged nut.

Using instructions

No2 sows 6 pints of Clover Seed per statute acre and   16 feet at cast. Or 2 bushels of Rye Grass to a statute acre and 16 feet at cast.

No3 sows 3 gallons of Flax or Trefoil to a statute acre and 12 feet at a cast.

No4 sows peeks of flax to a statute acre at a cast.

No5 sows 1 ½ bushels of Wheat to a statute acre and 24 feet at a cast.

No6 sows 2 ½ bushels Oats to a statute acre and 16 feet at a cast.

No7 sows 3 ½ bushels Oats to a statute acre and 16 feet at a cast. Or 3 bushels of Barley and 20 feet to a cast.

No8 sows 4 bushels Oats to a statute acre and 16 feet at a cast.

No9 sows 5 bushels Oats to a statute acre and 16 feet at a cast.

No10 sows 6 bushels Oats to a statute acre and 16 feet at a cast.

A shorter stick can be used for sowing headlands or narrow ridge Keep your seed clean Keep your belt tight. Oil the journals and grease the stick well. Keep a regular and firm motion. Never be entirely governed by the numbers as difference in the walk of the operator and the difference in quality of seed makes a gradual difference in the amount distributed therefore always measure in your hopper the amount of seed wanted of a cast or acre, and you will soon know how to set the machine to your walk, and never fail to get just the amount you want to the acre. This machine will also sow fertilizer.

I like the bit where you can sow fertilizer with it, and as for broadcasting 5 bushels of oats to the acre, the bag on top of the machine must only hold about half of a bushel.

Father always liked to broadcast by hand, for this he had a kidney shaped deep pan that had two loops and a vertical peg type handle.

Fine seed like kale, it was a finger and thumb job, and with

46

grain, in wet patches where it was too wet to get with the drill, it was hand full's at a time job.

It had a strap that went over his shoulder onto the two loops to carry it in front of him, this allowed him to use both hands swinging one hand then the other as a marching soldier, picking up seed at the front and slinging in a wide ark to distribute the seed with each stride.

I Remember the Seed Fiddle.
This happened in spring 1944 when I was 6 years old

Father he sowed the grass seed, with an old seed fiddle,
The field across the road, from house was all in stubble,
He filled up his fiddle, with grass seed and clover.
Seed bag as this end marker, his blue jacket at other,

Four yards move the marker, at each end of the bout,
March strait like a soldier, strides even and stout,
He pushed and pulled the bow, with each stride he took,
For the seed must spread thinly, according to the book.

Working through the morning, half the field is sown
He was heading for the sack, which he could sit down,
As a little lad to see my dad, went across the field,
Picked up his jacket on the way, look at me I squealed.

On seeing what I'd done, he wasn't very pleased,
He lost his far end marker, and with grass fine seed,
There was no way of telling, where he'd sown up to,
At very early age I learned, what the markers do.

It is like the seed put in the soil - the more one sows, the greater the harvest. Orison Swett Marden (1850-1924)

47

Chapter 9

The War-Ag had a stock of arable machinery.

Most tractors ran on petrol (gas), or started on petrol and run on TVO vaporizing oil (kerosene)

War time restrictions
During the Second World War, everyone suffered in some way or other, what with the food rationing, restrictions on fuel and most of the young men away at war.

Mechanization was just becoming popular in farming through necessity, in that a great push was on for the country to become self sufficient in food production.
Every farm had to compulsorily plough up some pasture to grow potatoes and wheat; in all the regions around the country the government (locally called the War-Ag) had a stock of arable machinery for those farms that had never grown arable crops before. It included tractors, usually the Standard Fordson, ploughs cultivators drills and harvesting equipment.

Fuel for road use was severely rationed, and most tractors ran on petrol, or started on petrol and run on TVO vaporizing oil the kind that we now call heating oil for central heating the house.
The petrol used on the farm was died red to prevent people from using it duty free on the roads, although it has been known for farm cars to run on a mixture that included a good proportion of TVO, you could always tell by the thin plume of light blue smoke emitted from the car exhaust.
Steel was a short commodity, metal and cast iron railings around buildings, and along the front of houses were

commandeered, On older houses even now there is often a low sandstone wall with the stumps of iron where the railing have been cut down.

Coal was another product in big demand; every house had fire places down stairs and up, and with electricity produced by coal fired power stations. Factories often had one big steam engine to run all the machinery; in steel works smelting was a big consumer that was essential. All the railway locomotives were steam up the main lines, transport also essential.

Allotments were provided for those with not much garden to help grow food for their own table, In a lot of back gardens there was a pig sty, particularly in the rural areas.

A piglet was purchased, and any household scraps, and edible garden waste, were fed to the pig that was eventually slaughtered. The carcass was quartered and salted, and hung up from a beam in the pantry. The bacon was sliced from the flitch by hand, and usually had as much fat as lean, when fried the pan was awash with fat , this was used to fry stale bread.

Always on the inside of the ribs of the pig was great quantities of leaf fat, this was rendered down to produce lard for cooking; the crackling that was left after the fat was drained off was very popular with the kids.

Pork pies were produced, to use up meat that was lower down the legs and the jelly formed from boiling the pigs trotters was poured into the pie through a small hole in the top, this excluded any air gaps after the pie was cooked.

The pigs head was boiled to produce brawn, when all the meat on the head was cooked and the bones lifted out, the water in the pot was further evaporated and reduced. The contents were then ladled into large basins and the top sealed, and a heavy weight place on top to compress it until cold.

This would keep for a while and then turned out onto a plate it was sliced brawn.

Milk was produced before the war using imported proteins such as linseed flakes, groundnut flakes and soya. These were the by-product of the vegetable oil crushers based in Liverpool; they also produced Astra soap at the Bibby's mill that also produced Dairy "cake" from the expeller flakes from crushing groundnut.

However when the U boats were sinking our ships in the Atlantic these products got into short supply, so it was essential to grow beans and peas. Occasionally they were grown as crops in there own right, but more often for cattle feed they were sown as "dredge corn". ,Oats wheat peas and beans all sown together , harvested when they all ripened , bindered ,stacked then threshed to produce an almost balanced ration for dairy cattle after it had been put through a roller mill.

Milking machines started to appear on farms due to the shortage of labor during the war, the milk was sent in churns to the towns and cities by train or by road transport. Some milk was made into butter and cheese on the farms and the whey fed to the pigs. Nothing was wasted.

Hens were found on every farm and in a lot of back gardens, most of them ran foraging about the yards and troughs around the buildings

It was important to watch where a clucking hen emerged from, and quite likely more than one would be laying eggs in that nest. So late in the afternoon you would go around with a bucket to collect the eggs from all the known nests. Nearly all the eggs were collected up once a week by the local Egg packing station, each wooden crate held twenty dozen eggs packed two and half dozen to the tray.

Some people preserved eggs in a preserving jell, and some eggs boiled hard then pickled in vinegar. Production of eggs tended to be seasonal; when the days and day light got short during winter they stopped lying. This was overcome to a certain extent it was found, by putting a light on in the hen house, so they would stay awake longer and eat more food from the feed hoppers and water fountains provided.

The following was in the 1950's before the days of combines. We had to collect the eggs from the field ark pens, into buckets. We hung the buckets on the handle bars of our bikes and rode down the main road from Bridgeford, about a quarter of a mile nearly all down hill. We got up to a fine turn of speed until one day I crashed with about twelve dozen eggs, these all broke across the road in front of Seighford Hall.

I had to explain what happened, but nobody cared about my skinned knees and elbows, mother was too concerned about all the eggs and income lost.

Mothers Laying Hens

Mother always kept,
A lot of laying hens,
Some in deep litter,
Some in field ark pens
Autumn they were put,
Onto far wheat stubble,
With pens on wheels,
Round the field did travel

Each pen held fifty hens,
They had slatted floors,
Nest boxes on each side,
Also flap down by the door,

51

Every two days they were moved,
For the hens to range,
Glean wheat that fell at harvest,
And to make a change.

Hens let out early morning,
And closed again at night,
There was plenty foxes,
To help themselves all right,
Eggs were collected every evening,
By the bucket full,
Plenty hay in which they lay,
Took it by the sackful.

On wet days with dirty feet,
Walked into the nest,
Left foot prints on the other eggs,
Oh what blooming pest,
With damp cloth we cleaned dirt off,
Worst ones we used Vim,
Took the bloom off them eggs,
View of packers would be dim

On dry days eggs were clean,
Onto sections packed,
Careful not to pack double yoked,
Or any that are cracked,
They were kept back for our breakfast,
Anything she tried,
Always nothing wasted,
Boiled or scrambled also fried.

Every Thursday lorry came,
Put out boxes in a dash,
Gave mother last weeks grading chit,
And her hard earned cash,
Sometimes she was very pleased,
Others disappointed,
Deductions made for small eggs,
And some that they had jilted.

So it was that these hens,
Came back in for winter,
In deep litter with light on,
Continued to lay to Easter,
Any falter or not look like lay,
They got their poor old neck rung,
Into boiling pot they went,
To feed her four hungry off-springs. (us lads)

. **Cheese – milk's leap towards immortality.**
Clifton Fadiman (1904-1999)

Chapter 10

Post and Rails of Oak

You don't see many fences now done with cleft oak post and rails, but I still have the wedges that we always used for the job. In case any younger generation have never seen it done, it's a way of splitting the oak trunk down into the required sizes along the grain of the wood.

Sawn rails where the grain waivers, and the saw crosses the grain that rail will split and break at the slightest push, and no matter how carefully the rails are sawn they cannot follow the grain exactly like you can with a cleft rail.

Posts are cleft the same, and for the corner or a gate post, they liked to have a post with a big knot where a branch had been cut off, this gave it a good anchor, with the heavy end in the ground.

When the rails were nailed onto the posts, they were fitted with the bark side down, it was like splitting an orange into segments, the narrow or pointed edge up turned the rain and they lasted longer.

The wheelwright and his brother would often split willow for rails, these did not last as long as oak, and were no good at all as posts, as in damp ground they would take root and grow on into a tree.

Willows were and still are a dam nuisance if they are any where near land drains, the fine roots matt up and fill the pipes for a good way beyond the canopy of the tree itself.

A new willow is started just by pushing in a willow stick in damp ground or on meadows it will strike instantly.

Father's Post and Rails of Oak

Father liked his fencing,
Post and rails of oak,
These will last a lifetime,
A very fussy bloke,
Usually on the boundary fence,
Everyone can see,
Up from where he laid his hedge,
Its how he learnt me.

Every now and then,
The estate would fell a tree,
Good straight trunk, cut into lengths,
For post and rails you see,
Six foot for the posts, ten for rails,
Wedges and hammer then,
Split the trunk each lump in half,
half and half again.

No waste at all, when you cleft
The trunk, all is utilized,
Looking at for what the job to do,
For thickness it is sized,
Posts dug in every nine foot;
Rails to fit are trimmed and perused,
These are always fitted; bark side down,
Rain it won't infuse.

First thing to go after standing for years
Is usually it's the nails,
They rust and go weak,
To the ground it drop the rails,

New nail needed but its not green oak,
Nails they soon bend,
Drill the rail, and nail it up,
Another decade of life extend.

There were few jobs father liked better than hedge laying, but he didn't always have much time to devote to it. He kept his own bill hook for that job hidden, so no one could spoil the edge that he had got on it, he had a holster that it went in when he was working.

There was an axe and brushing hook that he used on that job, also sharpened to perfection, a wooden mallet, knee pads and one left hand heavy leather mitten to protect from the thorns.

If it was a roadside hedge, it took twice as long to do as everyone passing stopped to talk and natter, but the pride he put into the job was beyond description.

It is only at the local Ploughing matches, that you see the older generation, working along side a few very keen youngsters, working to maintain this old craft.

I Remember Farther Hedge Laying

Father liked his hedge laying,
And every winter he,
Set about a big rough hedge
And stock proof it would be,
First he cut the hedge stakes,
In the wood where it was code, --- (cold)
Then to sharpen on a block,
On cart he would then load,

He honed his axe and bill hook,
To cut wood as if were carrot,
Put on his holster and leather glove,
Took a big wooden mallet,

He stripped the long tall growers,
Cleft them and also mention,
Always layer them up a slope,
And in the stakes were woven,

The top of his hedge was bound,
Like the top of a basket might,
He used long whippy willow strips,
Wove them firm and tight,
Burned up all the brushwood,
With a great big blazing fire,
Then he cleaned the ditch out,
And put up new barbed wire.

The new growth grew up through,
From stools all in the bottom,
A good dense hedge and stock proof,
Was the desired outcome,
Not need laying now for decade,
Till the gaps appear,
Then the master will return his skills
To make a new frontier.

The grass is not in fact, always greener on the other side of the fence. Fences have nothing to do with it. The grass is greenest where it is watered. When crossing over fences, carry water with you and tend the grass wherever you may be.

Robert Fulghum

Chapter 11

The Ploughing Match

There are usually classes for Open Vintage Trailed and Mounted, Classic Mounted, Novice and Open and World Style, Ferguson classes, and Garden tractors.

I Booked into a Ploughing Match

I booked into a ploughing match,
Their to show my skill,
See how straight and even,
My opening split instil,
A moment's loss of concentration
Blows the ideal apart,
Spend the rest of all that day,
Looking like upstart.

Good many tractors on the field,
All like minded to plough,
Markers out all over the place,
Beyond the plots allow,
Down and back complete the split;
Wait for judge to mark,
Close it up, flat top or pointed,
Critical watchers remark.

Some pause for lunch walk to see,
How the neighbours done,
Body language tells it all,
A grimace purse of lips so glum,

They try to break your confidence,
Concentration goes,
Look back and see plough blocked up,
New expletives compose.

All best mates when ya make a mess,
Condolence all come in,
A very polite clapping for best in class,
Everyone wishing to win,
A jolly good bunch of ploughmen,
Relax till judge comes back,
See who's is best of the bunch,
And who has got the plaque.

————————

The Elusive Cup

A disappointing outcome to a ploughing match using the
Fordson E27N and Elite plough for the first time.

Off to the ploughing match with great intent
Good weather help but the land is wet
Off down the field on the first run
Back up the second the twists begun.

Tipping in the third as though no skims
Blocking up the plough and the trouble begins
Coming up the fourth won't bury the stubble
Land wheel slipping and we're in trouble.

Off up the side of the neighbouring plot
Tape measure out to see what we've got
To start the cast it must be parallel
Or the finish, odd sized will give you hell.

Even furrows with good ins and outs
Firm for a seed bed well turned over each bout
No hand work or gardening is ever allowed
But it happens quite often when the judge turns around

To measure the land each bout is a must
As narrow it gets down to three or bust
The penultimate run is always shallow
It's to hold the plough firm as it turns its last furrow

Everyone's an expert who watches your last run
But get in the seat to feel how it's done
They block your eye line at the end of the stint
All standing astride, it's all wavering and bent

Everyone says we must not blame the tools
Not everyone there, that we can call fools
Experience shows by the polished plough
who puts it away with a tinge of rust now

Never again, and the thought that it's rotten
When the next one comes along and you've forgotten
Try once more for that elusive red card and cup
The knees will go weak, when ya eventually called up.

A day's work is a day's work, neither more nor less, and the man who does it needs a day's sustenance, a night's repose and due leisure, whether he be a painter or a ploughman.
George Bernard Shaw (1856-1950)

Chapter 12

Best loved Village character Tom Abbotts   born 1887

All the years I knew him,
He always had some wit,
Smoked a pipe and chewed Tabaco,
And showed us how to spit,
He had a bike sit-up-and beg,
Handle bars reached his chest,
On Friday went to town on it,
His hat he wore his best.

An old man, when I was a kid growing up, I can picture him now. This is what I remember of Tommy Abbotts in the 1940's & 50's when I was a lad growing up.

Tom Abbotts

Tom was born in 1887 and his sister Nellie in1893. As far as I know they had lived in Seighford possibly all there lives.

They lived in the back half of the large house, on the left on the way up to the airfield. The house had two fields that adjoined his garden and his buildings by the road not far from Tom's house.

He was an old man, when I was a boy in the late nineteen forties, and worked round the different farms in the village.

He kept two house cows to provide milk butter and cheese, and reared half a dozen calves. These he then grazed on one of his fields, the other field he kept shut up in the spring for hay.

These fields ran up to Bunns Bank and along to the next bend on the road onto the airfield the down almost to the Beeches Farm rickyard. In total he must have had about twelve acres, together with the small range of buildings on the road side with the G P O letter box built into its wall.

'Owd Tummy' as he was often called locally, was about five foot nine. He would stand with his right thumb in his waistcoat pocket, his left hand giving his pipe undivided attention. His feet would be at ten to two, and his weight evenly on both feet with his knees just forward of being locked (as you would stand in an earthquake).

He had a slight hump on his shoulders, and would carry his head be in the forward position as though ready for milking. This was his regular stance when looking at the cattle or when in deep thought, and when talking to neighbours. His face was always the same, a nose slightly narrow and pointed, and no extravagant expressions, almost what we call pan faced, But he only smiled with his eyes, I expect the pipe balked a big grin. His dark wide open eyes always seemed to sparkle, maybe because they often seemed to be wet, a good laugh and out with his hanky out of his pocket to dab them. Round his neck he nearly always had sweat band, to call it a ''neckerchief would be too posh and a cravat posher still. I've no doubt it was a habit from in the days when he used to break into a sweat. But these days he was a man who could pace himself and work at his own speed.

Quite a slim man in his time, but in the years, I knew him his trouser waist band had been modified by his sister Nellie, to cope with his expanding midriff, so discrete was this adjustment, that you could only see it when he bent over forward with the wind behind him, to blow his jacket up. She had cut the middle seam down the back of his trousers from the waist band about four inches, then the bracers buttons were put on the point of the opening, the fork of the bracers holding everything together comfortably.
His trousers were of a coarse tweed, and charcoal in colour with matching waste coat and jacket, clean but well worn, and modified as the years went on. The jacket had leather

patches on the elbows, and a strip sown on round the cuffs. The waistcoat was not outwardly modified but had stretched to the figure it contained, if anything had been done, it was ten or so buttons may have been brought up to edge of the material. A watch and chain stretched across the waistcoat into one pocket, the matches in the other, and tobacco pouch in his inside jacket pocket.

On the few occasions that his pipe was not in use it was stuffed in the top pocket of his jacket. More often than not it was in his teeth with his left arm hanging off it, with his first finger hanging over the bowl always ready to pack the tobacco if it went out.

He always had the same tobacco. It was twist which had to be rubbed before replenishing the pipe. The times when he was working with both hands, he would cut a piece of baccy with his pocket knife, pop it in his mouth and chew it. Every now and then he would have to eject some tobacco juice, with a long 'per-squit' which if it had been aimed to go somewhere. it always got there in a long unbroken stream..

He always wore boots, not a heavy type, but lighter sorts that would be polished from time to time. The boots had about ten lace holes and went well up above his ankles, almost to the calf of his leg. On working in the fields when there was mud about, he would wear some older boots and leather leggings.

To get about to fetch supplies and go to other farms, his only form of transport was his old bike, an old sit-up and beg type with rod brakes, twenty eight inch wheels. The handle bars were almost up to his chest when standing by it, and the seat as low as possible. It had a full chain case, and a carrier with a spring clip that would hold his Mac in case of rain, and around the hub of each wheel, inside of the spokes, was a loose small leather strap (like a small dog collar) to keep the hub bright and clean.

Each Friday he would go down to Stafford for his shopping, which was carried home in a carpet bag slung on his handle bars so deep was this bag that it hung right down to the middle of his front wheel. It certainly looked like a piece of carpet folded into two and stitched each side and with two cord handles which hung on the handle bars.

It was flat and hung flat, even when full it still hung flat. The only reason for going was to pick up a joint of beef from the butchers, and have a look in at the Sun Smithfield cattle market.

From the back door of his cottage you turned right, then left round the pear tree and another ten yards, you would be in the loo. A wooden seat with a bucket type, that had to be regularly attended to. (Emptied). A deep hole would be dug in the garden, and this would last about three months, filled over and then a new one dug.

Next to the loo was the pig sty, which most village houses had as standard, A single piglet was purchased when it was old enough to be weaned. Weaning took place when the sow was getting fed up with them, and the piglets would start chewing instead of sucking, and were eating in the trough with their mother. They would be fed on all sorts of house hold scraps like potato peelings, outer cabbage leaves and stalks, and only topped up with pig meal purchase from the corn merchant. On reaching maturity, the butcher would call and kill the pig and the flitches of bacon and hams cured by salting, these would be hung in a cool room in the house with a muslin bag over to keep the flies off.

Most of what they ate was home grown in the neat but large garden. , Everything would be preserved for winter. Potatoes and carrots dug and hogged, beetroot boiled and pickled, runner beans picked, sliced and salted, and packed in stone jars, plums and pears picked and preserved in kilner jars. Eggs were preserved in glycerine to seal the shells, would keep up to four months; eggs were also hard boiled and pickled. The only thing they bought seemed to be salt, coal, beef and bread.

They kept about twenty hens in a large run behind the pig sty , and it would be disaster if the hens got loose in the garden, these were kept for eggs and for eating and hatching.

All the cattle were reared from calves by Nellie, named and thoroughly spoiled; they could almost milk them in the middle of the field. When it came to sell them, it was more traumatic than they let on; it was as if one of the family leaving home for good.

On a large proportion of the garden Tommy grew mangols (mangol wursels) .These were pulled and topped and taken into one of his sheds to protect them from the frost, to feed to the older cattle through the winter. Hay was the other main feed; this was cut in early July by one of the neighbours who he had worked for during the spring, quite often my father. The hay would be turned and tedded with great care for four days, and if the weather held good, father would bale it. This would be after 1958 when balers first came out before this date it would be carried and stacked loose.

Us lads, and the cow man and the Wagoner (now called the tractor driver) would all go round, cart it and stack it in his yard , Tom would do the supervising in the pose I described above Nellie brought the large enamel gallon jug of tea, with a handful of cups and mugs. Everyone with cup in hand held steady for Nellie to pour out the welcome tea Philip the cowman had a sip, and as Nellie and Tom turned away round the stack Philip dashed his tea under the hedge.

On her return Nellie topped his mug up again, Philip thanking her and complimenting her on the tea, but the same thing happened, it was dashed under the hedge again discretely.

My brothers and I saw all what went on, and when Nellie had collected up the cup and had gone back to the house, we enquired why no tea? Being an experienced cowman, he had observed that the only cow Tom had in milk at that time, had only calved the day before. That meant that the rich creamy tea had been made with beestings, this he could not stomach. Nellie being very thrifty, in her mind had made a good milky brew.

Beestings are produced by the cow for the first four days of lactating and they contain antibodies to protect the calf. They are extra rich to nourish a new born calf from birth. If beestings from the second milking are put in a large flat basin and put in the oven to slowly cook on low heat for an hour and a half, with a bit of nutmeg on top it comes out set like custard. Very nice hot or cold for pudding, and very popular with us kids (but not in tea)

Tom and Nellie were very private people, very few went into the house. It was like stepping back in time, even in the 1950`s. Then all of a sudden they bought a television and a long tall aerial was mounted on the tallest chimney.

As they got older they gave up the land and sold the cattle .The garden was getting too much for him, cultivating it less each year. Then in 1963 at the age of 70, Nellie died, Tom had relied on Nellie for the cooking and washing, and coped on his own remarkably well until he was finding it difficult to get about especially in the winter months.

The neighbours were alert to his situation, and someone called on him every day to do his bit of washing, get the coal in and chop the sticks for fire lighting etc. He had no immediate family as neither of them had ever been married. The only relatives lived a long way off. Then in 1977 Tom died at the age of 90. He remained cheerful, and great fun to all who knew him. He had been like this all his life. He was a man who never raised his voice or lost his temper, a very shy man with strangers.

A man of few words, and good listener, although his face did not show it, he was a very jovial man who enjoyed a good joke, but seldom did he ever tell one.

His grave was dug and the coffin made by the village
wheelwright and his brother, Jim and Bill Clark, as was
Nellie's. Bill was grave digger and Jim made the coffins.
Tom and Nellie's grave is near the top step of the back lane
path of St 'Chad's church, among other old characters and
residents of Seighford

Owed Tom Abbotts

Owed Tom Abbotts lived in a cottage,
With his sister Nell,
They kept three cows and calves,
And a few old hens as well,
Cattle grazed across four acres,
The rest was mown for hay,
In his garden he grew his mangols,
Fed in short winters day.

He helped his neighbors,
When they're short handed,
With drilling hoeing weeding,
With others he was banded,
At harvest time he stacked bays,
Till in the roof was bound,
Longest ladder then was cast,
Him get back to ground.

All the years I knew him,
He always had some wit,
Smoked a pipe and chewed tobacco,
And showed us how to spit,
He had a bike sit-up-and beg,
Handle bars reached his chest,
On Friday went to town on it,
His hat he wore his best.

His shopping bag hung on his bike,
A long carpet bag it was,
All stitched up on either side,
Flat by front wheel because,
When it was loaded it was safe,
Hung by strong loops of cord,
Should it be carried in his hand,
It almost dragged with the hoard.

As a young man stood up straight,
He'd be all of five foot eight,
Old and stooped and round of back,
Shorter still as life dictate,
Feet a splayed for easy stance,
And knees a slight of bend,
One thumb hooked in waist coat pocket,
Tuther to pipe distend.

He always had a cheery smile,
His eyes were almost closed,
When he had a dam good laugh,
Tears ran down his pointed nose,
His face was brown and ruddy,
From working in all weathers,
On his nose and chin could see,
Red veins mapped his features.

On his feet were black boots,
Well up above his ankle laced,
His trousers had a gusset,
Hold his expanding tummy braced,
It was a different colour,
And could see when he bent over,
And buttons of his bracers,
Straining hard to cotton anchor.

Waistcoat matched his trousers,
A suit some point decide,
Ten buttons some were missing,
Four pockets two each side,
One it held his pocket watch,
Secured to button hole with chain,
Another held his match box,
England's Glory was it by name.

His jacket didn't quite match,
Been stitched around the collar,
Pockets drooped like open mouth,
Weighed down as if to cower,
In one was his bacca pouch,
Top pocket reserved for pipe,
Pipe was mostly in his mouth,
Not always did he light.

He carried a little pocket knife,
His baccy Twist to cut,
When he rubbed it in his palm,
Into his pipe he put,
With cupped hand around his pipe,
He lit it with a match,
Puff and suck till it was lit,
Mid curls of smoke detach.

Eventually it went out again,
And back into top pocket,
Out with the Twist and cut a knob,
Chew into old tooth socket,
This is where he taught all us kids,
To squit with baccy juice,
It went with long streak so far,
To reach his poor old goose.

Tommy had a bowler hat,
Kept on peg inside of his back door,
As kids he let us try it on,
And asked him what it was for,
It was used to go to town in,
Now for only funerals touted,
He kept it brushed and steamed,
Though it became out dated.

.Now it was only flat caps,
That he was nare without,
Into town he used his best,
To walk around see who's about,
One was used to milk his cows,
Grease and cow muck plastered
And one used round house and village,
Not so much it mattered.

Tommy's ears were large and thin,
For a man so short,
Ragged round the top edge,
Frost bite they must have caught,
They tucked back nice and even,
His cap they're there to hold,
His head he kept it nice and warm,
Ears out in the cold.

His garden always nicely dug,
And cow muck spread a plenty,
Grew his household veg and spuds,
And runner beans a bounty,
The biggest plot was that of mangols,
For his pampered cows,
The three of them all bedded up,
Roots chopped for them to brows.

We called round my dad and me,
And Nelly made us a cup of tea,
One of Tom's cows had calved,
The others had dried off you see,
Milk she poured all rich and yellow,
Beestings from his old cow,
She had to stir most vigorously,
Tea too rich to drink right now.

In winter time when he was younger,
Tom he carted coal,
Picked it up from Bridgeford Station,
Seighford was his goal,
Brought it over Bridgeford bank,
With donkey and a cart,
This it filled the time o'er winter,
Before drilling corn did start.

So it was that he got too old,
To work about the farms,
Even gave up his cows and garden,
That he loved and charmed,
Then he lost his sister Nell,
And lived a few more years alone,
He himself succumbed to life,
Both still in Seighford neath headstone.

I Remember Singling Sugar Beet

I remember singling sugar beet,
On Barn Field it was long,
Ten of us following close,
And talking in a throng,
Owd Tommy he was slow,
And he got left behind,
Ground was dry and dusty,
Not enough to blind.

Now George he's in his thirties,
His bladder wouldn't hold,
Got to have a pee now,
Halfway down the row behold,
He pee'd on top of Tommy's row,
And then he carried on,
Till Tommy came across a damp spot,
In his row dead on.

Further down we all watched,
As he stuck his finger in,
To see what had wet the earth,
Held muddy finger by his chin,
We all rolled with laughter,
Till we told him what was on his paws,
Poor Owd Tummy takes a joke,
Short straw he always draws.

**Young men, hear an old man to whom old men harkened
when he was young.**
Ceasar Augustus (63 BC -14 AD)

Chapter 13

We Had a Woodwork Teacher

If he could not get class attention, throw a chisel hard,
Hit the back wall cupboard, like a dagger stuck and jarred.

After our formative year at the small village school, it came as a shock to mix with such huge groups of kids, (over 600) a big proportion town kids, some showing aggression to us village kids.

But we soon realised that they could only do that when they out numbered us, and one good BOOO at them was enough to stand them back.

We had always been used to working in school in one classroom, but hear we all had to up sticks and move round to specialist classrooms that dealt with a particular subject. The classes I liked most were the woodwork and metalwork classes, although the two teachers could not have been more different.

Harry Nuttall was the metalwork teacher, he always seemed to me to be a bit short sighted as he wore heavy thick lens glasses, and a brown smock, he showed us how to mark out with a scribe in sheet metal, the first thing to make was a round washer and a square washer, going along the scribe marks with the centre punch making a row of small dots to file the metal down to the size marked.

Then we made a fire poker with a loop top to hang it up, progressing on to a brass toasting fork, and on to make a fancy bowl out of copper, first rubbing it with soap the heating it to soften it until the soap went black, more heat and it would melt. Next we hammered it with a planishing hammer on a leather cushion full of sand, gently hammering round and round and starting to hollow the centre. Rub with soap again and soften it again, repeating until it was rely hollowed out.

Then we cut a bit of round brass rod and formed it into a circle and soldered it in the bottom so it would stand firm, and the same again round the top edge and the finished thing was buffed up and highly polished on an electric mop.

Mr Leese was the woodwork teacher, and because he wore a permanent scowl we called him Bulldog Leese. He showed us how to use a set square and scribe and how to saw a piece of wood following the pencil marks. Not being used to sharp saws we had the habit of putting pressure on the blade as you worked like cutting logs at home, but with his saws we were told in no uncertain terms that the weight of the saw was all that was needed.

We learned how to make all the popular joint and dovetails and to match one lump of wood to fit exactly into the other then glue to make a firm elbow.

Some kids just could not get the idea of sawing straight, and Bulldog would not let them progress until they could. The same when using the plane, to keep it flat on the timber right to the end, and not let it tip as it went over the far end.

Chisels of all sizes (he had twenty of every tool needed in woodwork lessons), these were kept in tall cupboards at the back of the class room hanging in rows on the inside of the doors.

Mortars and tenant joints were carved out with chisels so sharp and almost too dangerous for kids to use.

Again there was always one or two who just could not do the job no matter how they tried, and this wound him up into such a rage. In fact to impress on us who was boss and who we had got to listen to he threw a chisel from where he stood at the front of the class, at the cupboard on the back wall in his frustration so hard it jarred like a dagger in the door.

Nowadays he would have been dragged in front of the courts and suspended on full pay indefinably, but it was his way of making sure we listened.

We Had a Woodwork Teacher (1950 ish)

We had a woodwork teacher, called him Bulldog Leese,
Had stern face and bad temper, no one dare to tease,
If he could not get class attention, throw a chisel hard,
Hit back wall cupboard, like a dagger stuck and jarred.

All the class stood and quivered dare not cross his path,
The respect was thrust upon you; dare not stir his wrath,
No one liked his class even those who could push a plane,
Perfection in this man and all his tools, but he was a
bloody pain.

Men are like steel. When they loose their temper, they loose their worth.
Chuck Norris (1940-)

The School Bus

Austin's service busses ran from Woodseaves via Seighford to Stafford and took us kids to the BIG school in 1950's.
We (our village) were on the westerly route out of town; it

was this same bus company that ran a service to the southerly route of the county town.

6.00 pm was the last bus for anyone working in town to get home on that southerly route, so it was always full to bursting, in fact the police one night noticed how badly that double decker was sagging in its springs and on the corners listed and leaned over with the weight.

So on top of Billington bank, after the bus had struggled up to the top the police pounced and inspected its load. The bus supposed to carry fifty two seated, when the police unloaded the bus they had counted one hundred and ten. This was widely reported in all the papers and the bus company fined for over loading. It became a rule that they could put as many as they can cram on, on the bottom deck, and seated only up top.

If you look at the normal London double Decker bus, the top deck has an isle down the centre, with six foot headroom, but these worn out utility type of bus had been built specially for a bus company up north where they had some bridges that would not take the full height bus.

They were a good foot and a half lower, this was achieved by putting in a sunken isle along one side of the upper deck, the long bench type seats to take four people which had to be reached by ducking low along the seat, on sitting down there was just enough headroom to be comfortable.

On the deck below the person who sat under this side isle had it almost touching their head. Our local bus company had bought a few of these worn out busses second hand, so you can see why they were so unstable, all the upper deck was loaded to the left hand side, and driving on the left as we do , the country roads always had a fair camber to the left.

Going round some of the right hand corners with a left hand camber and a left hand load it looked a bit scary, as the bus buried its rear left wheel well up into its wheel arch. Don't think they had invented anti-roll bar in them days.

Our gang from Seighford always sat at the front upstairs and aggravated the driver by banging our feet on the floor above his head. Some drivers took no notice but.

Tommy M. our regular driver at that time, got very annoyed, and on our route home, he ran the bus onto the grass verge and under some low over hanging branches of a tree.

These buses running the rural route had dents in the top front panels anyway, so a few more made no difference. Playing about as we did and banging the floor, and not looking where we were going it came as a terrible shock to us as the twigs and light braches crashed the font windows at full speed.

It did settle us down for a week or two, as we watched where we were going to be ready next time he pulled that trick.

However the stamping on the floor began again, and out in the country on a down hill slope he jammed on his brakes , jumped out of his cab, round to the back of his bus and came upstairs two at a time and faced us in a very agitated threatening manor. Of course we sat very innocently, but were trapped where we sat, as he stood shaking with rage in the sunken passage of the upper deck.

Tommy was normally quite jovial type of chap with a terrible sssssstuter, and would take quite a time to get out of his mouth what he had got to say. But on this occasion, he was a different man, all his cursing language came flooding out loud and clear for all to hear, and not a stutter to be heard.

The rest of the journey home he drove very erratically, and we paid full attention trying to anticipate which way to lean on the corners, so as not to be chucked about.

A couple of years on and Tommy got another job, it was with our threshing contractor as a mate to the driver of the threshing set. His stutter had not improved at all, and he often recalled the times of when we aggravated him on his bus. Who knows he may have been bated by other lads on other routes, but he got fed up and found another job.

Tommy the School Bus Driver

Each day we travelled off to the big school,
Caught the bus at a stop by the farm as a rule,
It was a service bus, tired old double Decker,
Second hand, and looked like an old wrecker.

We all had passes, and didn't have to pay,
Supposed to show, them every day,
Inspector shows up, every now and then,
Lost our passes, and out with his pen.

Threaten to put us off, going in to school,
Were very pleased, but pretend it's cruel,
A different matter, on the way home,
Delaying tactics, till a pass I loan.

On the upper deck, right at the front,
Our gang filled seats, swayed with the movement,
We stamped our feet, bov the drivers head,
Then looked out the window, at what's coming ahead.

Driver took bus, along the grass verge,
And under low branch, of a tree with a surge,
It rattled the front window, and roof of the bus,
We dived for cover; under the seats he's reckless.

For quite a few weeks, with that driver on,
It was quiet up top, till thought we'd test this moron,
Stamping again, over his head,
He put the brakes, on and stopped it dead.

Tommy the driver, got out of his cab,
Shot round the back, hand rail did grab,
Off up the stairs, and up to the front,
Shouted and shouted, he was most blunt.

Tommy had got a most terrible s-s-s-stutter,
He blinked his eyes, and looked down to the gutter,
Eventually his words came out with a rush,
Had to listen carefully, when he was in full flush.

On this afternoon, on the way home,
In his anger he forgot, all about his syndrome,
His words came out, flooding and direct,
His words were perfect, no stutter detect.

81

We thought we had cured him, a relief it was,
To this poor man's stutter, we had the cause,
When he had calmed down, on the next day,
His stutter was back, and he was okay.

Some times as a stunt, he would drive past our farm,
Make us walk back, to cause us alarm,
But we didn't mind, some old lady we'd find,
Had got to walk back, driver's name she maligned.

Got to know Tommy, good driver he was,
Always waved and piped, on way by in his bus,
He never did get rid, of his terrible stutter,
Was how he's made when, he wanted to chatter.

————————

**Knowledge and timber shouldn't be much
used till they are seasoned.**
Oliver Wendell Holmes.

Chapter 14

Family Tree back to 1753

I am second of four, father was eldest of four, grandfather was one of eight, G. grandfather was youngest of seven, G.G. grandfather was youngest of eight, and my G.G.G. grandfather was born in 1753

In these modern days of computers and search engines like Google, it makes it relatively easy to follow back into records that you may never have known exist, all done from the comfort of a chair. There are a few relatives that we have been in touch with who we may never otherwise have known, and there are far more folk doing their family tree than you would ever expect.
Its only when you find someone on a distant branch of your own tree that they can be merged to fill out a broader picture.

Looking at very old wedding groups, to see and realise that the little lad sitting cross legged in the front row was your grandfather, and the old and stern lady with a bun hair do and a hat sitting on top was his mother. Then sorting out the two sets of grand parents and the four sets of great grand parents, not necessarily in the same photograph, it gets confusing, and they all have the habit of dying at widely different ages, and between one group photo and the next, some go missing and some new ones born.
Half the job involves looking round church yards reading information off the grave stones, and even in our case an engraved stone in the pub next door, he must have been a very good customer or owned the pub as well as farmed next to the church.

Out of the six generations of farmers, myself and my father

were the only ones to benefit from the use of tractors, prior to that the modern or new machinery would be the binder for cutting and tying the shoffs of corn, and the horse drawn mowing machine to replace cutting grass with the scythe. The Ginny ring to convert horse power into a rotating shaft in turn to power barn machinery, a winnower to separate the grain from the chaff, and grain would be taken down to the wind mill or water mill, for grinding into flour.

Eventually a barn engine would be installed to drive a line of shafting connecting all the barn machinery to this one engine, usually (this is in my time) it was a root cutter and cleaner, a chaff cutter, a cake crusher, and a grinding mill.

A quarter of the farms land would be to feed the horse's, oats and the straw for bedding, plus a handy field of turf to turn them out at night, and enough grass land to make hay for them. A work horse can eat as much hay as two cows, so total farm output was severely diminished.

Man power was abundant, and a hundred and forty acre farm would have five or six men working outside round the farm, (now it's barley able to support one man in work and income), the younger single male workers living in, in the farm house, then in the farm house would a number of women making butter and cheese and other menial house hold chores.

There is still evidence in our house where the lodgers or farm lads used to live, they had a back stair case and one room upstairs, the walls were always of lime wash. A dividing door on the landing up stairs was kept bolted from the farmer's side; this enabled him to ensure they got up early, every morning

I heard tell from a chap who used to live in such accommodation that they lived on rabbit pie seven days a week and milk puddings and porridge oats, presumably snaffled from under the horses feed store.

He said he had never had rabbit pie from the day he left that farm till the day he dies, such was the misery that some of them endured as young farm servants.

Some families, like us stayed rooted within a few miles from where they were "dropped", marrying local, some strayed and spread all over the country. We have one lad born in 1840 who went to Australia and another who went to USA in the 1880's and had four children out there, so no doubt we should have relatives to find and visit world wide.
Of coarse there is, as in every family, the odd ones who we would prefer not to mention by name, such as the one who got a little thirsty (living next to the pub, or did he own it?) One who married a girl of sixteen after already having a child by him in the 1860's; they did go on to have another six children one of which was my grandfather.

I am the second of four, my father was eldest of four, my grandfather was one of eight, G. grandfather was youngest one of seven, G.G. grandfather was youngest of eight, and my G.G.G. grandfather was born in 1753, not found his family out yet but it is getting more difficult as you get that far back.

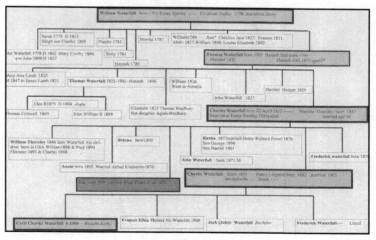

The yellow block bottom left is my father, next up is Grandfather, and next up is Great grandfather, up again is GG grandfather and at the top is GGG grandfather born in 1753 at Fenny Bentley, Derbyshire

Not started mothers side of the family yet but she was one of nine, being a twin they were seventh and eighth born, so they will be an interesting search back into the great grand parents.

Mother's mother lost her husband soon after the last one was born, and had a farm to run, the eldest ones helped, but we were told grandma would often be seen out ploughing with a pair of shires, she was a big strong women of six foot, I remember her as not quite so tall being a little bent with age and labour.

Grandma also was a big "Chapel" organist (in a little Chapel), pumping the organ vigorously with her feet and singing very loudly, and then the Chapel did only hold about twenty, and all the kids had to attend twice every Sunday.

So as you see, it will occupy many hour of time and searching, and visiting the different houses and farms that they had occupied at some time in the past, plus the church yards where they were finally laid to rest.

A family wedding photograph in front of Littywood Manor in 1872. This was the farm that our family moved to down from Fenny Bentley in Derbyshire.
"Google" "Littywood" Stafford, on the computer to see its up to date pictures of it now.

Our Family Tree

A family tree were working on,
To see from where we came,
Of people who we never knew,
We all have the same name,
We all remember our own grandma
And grandpa as well,
But they remember their old folk,
A tale of old to tell.

Big families of eight or nine,
And some they lost quite young,
Some they stayed as spinsters
Or bachelors un sung,
Working on estates and farms,
In houses cold and damp
Some on their own farms,
On land their mark to stamp.

Looking back on old grave stones,
Name chiselled bold and clear,
Got to look where they're christened
Who their parents were,
Who they met and married,
The families joined and spread,
The kids that came along so quick,
Along same paths we tread.

We scour along old census records
From many years gone by,
See the age of head of household
And all who lived and why,
Some left home at early age
For to find some work,
Spread around the villages,
None of them to shirk

Need a bigger sheet of paper,
As the families spread and grow,
William Thomas Charles and John,
Reoccur in all lines we know.
Now were back to where were found,
Back to 1753 we tow,
Following all the records of,
The church and census as we go.

Our turn will come soon enough,
As time it flashes by,
Never know when that will be,
Its better laugh than cry,
Name and date of birth and death,
Chiselled into stone,
A patch of good old England,
Neath turf that's our last home.

It's easier to put on slippers than to carpet the whole world.
Al Franken

Chapter 15

Gardening

The roses get the green fly, the taters get the blight,
The cabbage get the caterpillars, what a blooming sight,

A gardening Story

Many potential gardeners who work, and travel some distance to and from work, just physically do not have much time to do what they would like to do in the garden.

Then there is the people who just cannot stand gardening, like a neighbour we had in the village, (the wheelwright), his wife loved her garden, and he was committed to mowing the lawns front and back, and always commented to who ever would listen, that his garden should be tarmac end to end, side to side, then each spring he could just sweep it off and paint it green.

This was about the time they were building the new M6 motorway, and different "cowboy" contractors were "peddling" tarmac at night and weekends, to do the drive or garden paths, at a rate never to beaten, cash only, right into their back pockets.

However his wife would not here of it, and they kept to lawns and boarders on the front and a veg. plot and some lawn at the back of the house.

This is how I sum up gardening

Gardening as a Pastime

The lawns are mowed the grass removed,
Starve it if you can,
Start in March or sooner,
Cut it twice a week's the plan,

Grows like mad till the summer,
Then brown and crusty goes,
Precious water sprinkled on,
The time and cost who knows.

Had the mower sharpened,
Through mole hills it has cut,
They're only after earth worms,
To fill their little gut,
Got to have a blow hole,
To push the soil out,
Maize of tunnels under the lawn,
So tough and black and stout.

The roses get the green fly,
The taters get the blight
The cabbage get the caterpillars,
What a blooming sight,
Apples there are plenty,
Grub hole in every one,
Birds have pecked the plums,
The rot it has begun.

The wasps are round the jam pot,
Flies around the meat,
Its summertime enjoy it,
Try getting out the heat,
Cooler in the evenings,
Sit in the garden to relax,
Midges bite your arms and legs,
Round ya head attacks.

Cut the hedge about three times,
Clearing up the leaves,
Hawthorne holly and brambles,
Full of thorns it heaves,
Fingers sore and bleeding,
Enjoy the job they say,
Out in fresh air and sunshine,
All this work no pay.

Nettles in the corners,
Tackle then if you dare,
Just the lightest touch from one,
It'll make you swear,
Cut they come again times ten,
Fresh and green as ever,
Save them for the butterflies,
Neglect'll mek ya look clever.

Green fingers what a laugh,
Muck builds up under nails,
It keeps you fit and healthy,
Keeps ya weight off the scales,
Organically grown is good for you,
But pests they are a pest,
Work with nature is what they say;
You can only do your best.

———————

This (below) is the bit the misses looks after and is in charge of, were both getting no younger and the veg garden went some years ago. Its trim the lawn, trim the bushes, cut the hedge (with the tractor flail hedge cutter I can manage that job well) boarders and bedding plants to the minimum, just enough to give a bit of colour and interest.

This is my effort on the yard in an old concrete water trough.

No farmer ever looks at the flowers twice, but study what in the background, an old upturned grain hopper, five bays filled with HAY, and some haylage under cover, silage bales are stacked outside out of the picture.

My loader will only reach to stack three bales high, that's it on the Agrotron in the background, and the hedge cutter on the Fastrac. The old barn legs have started rotting and have had a tump of concrete two foot up the legs.

Standing parked between the green tractor and the barn, the Landrover flat trailer with an old three furrow Fordson Elite Plough.

This is just a farmer's view of a tub of flowers, one line of writing for the flowers, and six lines for the background, think that's pretty normal.

Around the 1960's it was fashionable to sow turnips from the air in June /July into the standing crops of corn, (wheat barley or oats). In this case it was barley, and the top end of the field was a single cottage, folks came out of their village houses to watch the aerobatics as the plane swooped low over the crop, dodging hedge row trees, then up almost vertical, turn and back down for the next run.

The man in the cottage watched as it swooped and turned short of his house, having got a grandstand seat so to speak. In the next few months the crop of barley was combined, and the rain and moisture had germinated a good stand of turnips in the stubble, trouble was the cottage garden had also got turnips growing in the garden, and worse still, a full and vigorous crop was growing in the gutters and spouting all round the house.

Of coarse when the seed was being dropped no one knew why he was diving and swooping and the turnip seed is so fine and no dust trail as the seed fell.

It was only a few years that that aerial spreading of seeds and sprays lasted, as the drift into adjoining fields and crops, and houses brought it to be banned, so the turnips sprouting in the spouting only happened the one year in our village.

This same cottage, the occupant often went to the local market to take eggs to sell, often a sitting of hen and bantam eggs. It was in the spring he came home with a sitting of goose eggs, and set them under a couple of broody hens, they duly hatched and rapidly grew bigger than the old mother hen, they started running and flapping their wings when they were loosed out in the mornings , as geese do.

Then to his amazement one morning they took off, and flew round and landed back in the garden, soon they flew off for half an hour or more but always came back.

The sitting of eggs he had bought were that of Canadian Geese, and in the autumn one morning they took off and he never saw them again. No goose for Christmas for him.

This shows off the detailed workmanship that went into the old wicket (gate) made by the old blacksmiths of years ago.

If there is no gardener there is no garden
Stephen Cov

Chapter 16

The British Hedgerows and Boundaries.

The fields both large and small have names,
You wouldn't dream exist,
Some relate to owner past,
And others the type of land persists,

It seem most important to British people that their Boundaries are marked by a fence or ditch and hedgerow or both. It is also important to know who's responsible for its maintenance and repair.

On farms it is your own responsibility to keep your own cattle contained within your boundary. Having said that, in the early days you marked your boundary by digging a ditch along your side of the line, and throwing the spoil back into your own side, then plant a hedge on top of it. In other words it's your boundary if the ditch is the other side of the hedge or fence. Internal ditches were often dug and a hedge planted, to pick up springs and tile drains that crossed the farm, and clear storm water to prevent shallow pools forming, which would kill the grass after a few week submerged.

Very old hedgerows are often made up of many species, ranging from Hawthorn and Blackthorn to Brier and Elder, the latter two being not very desirable, as livestock tend to eat through them. Unless the hedges are trimmed each year they soon become open in the bottom, and very loose in the top. Hawthorn and Holly make a good tight knit defence against cattle, but can soon become gappy when Elder which is a quick grower becomes dominant. Then when livestock are turned into the field, they eat it.

In one of our hedges, a botanist counted over twenty different species of hedgerow plant in a hundred yard stretch. This is a hedge that had evolved over the years in a grazing pasture, where cattle have made their contribution to pruning. Only the less palatable species dominated and maintained quite a good hedge.

Often the best trees to grow from saplings are the ones that are growing in the hedge bottom, when they appear out of the top of the hedge they can just be cut round and simply left to grow. No problem of transplanting or guarding they grow on to make splendid trees with no setbacks.

Hedgerows are important to birds, for nesting and for berries for winter feeding, and the hedge bottom, is shelter for a wide range of small mammals.

The ideal hedge, I was told, over fifty years ago, should be A shaped, and when in full leaf sheds rain like a thatched roof.

This gives maximum shelter to its inhabitants, and a wide and dry undisturbed hedge bottom, , and a build-up of dry leaf mould, for hibernating wildlife like Hedgehogs and Toads. Rabbits like to burrow under hedges, as very often the soil is relatively loose and not too compacted, the roots of the hedge also hold the burrow open, and no danger of collapse. Also growing on top of a small hedge bank, it is well drained and dry.

Badgers often dig in old rabbit warrens; particularly if they hit a good seam of sand that is just below a hard gravely layer. Here they can dig rapidly forming great mounds of sand that could turn a tractor over, if you're not concentrating.

Field mice and voles find shelter in the hedge banks, running among the tussocks of grass. At harvest time they venture further out in the field margins foraging for shed grain, where they fall pray to the kestrels and buzzards. When they spot a mouse, they hover then dive, carrying them off in their talons, owls too like this type of habitat.

On our estate fifty years ago, the woodman when needed

would cut down an oak tree. The main trunk would be cut into a 5ft 6in length and 10ft length and multiples of that to make best use of the tree trunk. These large sections of tree trunk were then cleft (split) with wedges and a sledge hammer to make fencing posts and the longer ones into rails. This practice is never used nowadays, but cleft timber was always better and stronger than sawn timber. This was because split timber always followed the grain of the wood, and sawn timber inevitably crossed the grain somewhere along its length and could break in that place. There are still examples of cleft posts and rails in parts of the estate but they are getting few and far between.

In the Moor Cover wood there always used to be a section in the lower part of the wood that was coppiced. The stools that had been harvested two or three years before were again ready to be cut. The most common use was for hedge laying stakes, and the whippy tops used to bind the top of the laid hedge. When completed this binding would look like the top edge of a basket, holding the light stakes and laid hedge stiff, durable and stock proof. Another use of the lighter stakes was for thatching pegs, these needed to be about 2ft long the thicker ones would be cleft into two, they would then be sharpened at one end to make it easier to push into the stack of hay or corn.

The brash left after coppicing found it way into many of the village gardens as pea and bean sticks, and no opportunity was lost on finding a new seven or eight foot cloths line prop with a natural forked top.

Field Names of Seighford

Out in Britons countryside,
Looks like a patchwork quilt,
Of roads and lanes and field tracks,
Evolved and some were built,
They lead from towns and villages,
And farms, map nailed on beam,
Each field a hedge and ditch and gate,
Watered by pond or stream.

The fields both large and small have names,
you wouldn't dream exist,
Some relate to owner past,
And others the type of land persists,
Red Rheine's is one of these mean fields,
When ploughed reveals red clay,
Unless the frost gets into it,
No seed bed though you work all day.

Best known one I've no doubt,
Behind Yews farm is Cumbers,
Ten houses built along the village,
Take that name and numbers,

Down by the ford is Mill Bank,
Four acre few trees by the brook,
The Hazel Graze another great name,
Nut bushes to make a crook.

Fosters by the railway line,
Named after a soul long gone,
And Pingles also down the Moor Lane,
That defiantly is a mystery one,
Noons Birch is the most beautiful name,
One that congers' you mind,
Public Field it was part of the land,
Run to the pub up back and behind.

Hobble End is another nice name,
Where two cottages stood in the fields,
No track did they only footpath,
Lonely place only a well and concealed,
Moss Common a field where the ditch,
Springs in the middle to pick up,
It is important that they are there,
To water the ewes and the tup.

Ash Pits are three fields in a row,
The Big the Middle and Little,
Ash trees are the obvious reason,
And only one pit in the lot,
Hanging Bank is most sinister name,
It's a cold north facing bank,
More research into this is what's needed,
But all we've drawn is a blank

Lanes to the fields also have names,
Moor Lane runs way from the ford,
Connecting with that is Love Lane,
A grassy rut track half way Bridgeford,
The Oldfords Lane goes up to the farm,
To Coton not a short cut by car,
And Smithy Lane runs way through houses,
the shortest of all by far.

Moss Lane is one that runs eastwards,
Cow lane that it is can be seen,
Grass up the middle and is long,
See cattle grazing fields so keen,
It has path that runs up it,
And gates shut on each end,
The path is quite long;
It comes out near Doxey on bend.

**If we had no winter, the spring would not be so pleasant,
if we did not sometimes taste adversity, prosperity would
not be so welcome.**
Anne Bradstreet (1612-1672)

Chapter 17

Life does not get any easier

After around three or four minuets cutting, the bulls horn eventually dropped off, a nice clean cut but we had three spurts of blood,

Life does not get any easier, what with the budget and the economy, and nearer to home we had two cows lost the calves at birth, and looks like the cow lay still, with the veil over the calf's nose and suffocated it. Also to make up the numbers a cow had twins, of coarse it had to be the oldest and thinnest cow, the one to be run baron this time and culled.

So we are in the throws of settling one of the twins onto one of these cows, so far she is taking to it well. The second cow to loose her calf I have bought in a calf off a neighbour, but she is an angry cow, and she has a pair of sharp horns and knows how to use them on her companion (the first cow to loose her calf).

We have often said that the horns aught to come off, but as a suckler cow living out all the year round there was no need to have the operation.

In order that we can hold her long enough and still enough for the new calf to suckle, we have borrowed a neighbours crush, it has side panels that open to let the calf suck, ours has solid sides. Being such a strong crush, and seeing as how she had drawn blood and gashed her companion quite viciously, we decided that the horns can come off NOW.

Injection to numb the base of the horn, count to a hundred and one slowly, and cut them off promptly with a wire. So quick and efficiently with hardly any blood, we looked who else qualified to have the same opp.

And there he was, the bull, standing quietly by the gate,

opened it and he walked through, and voluntarily walked as far as he could down the race and got stuck in the first half of the crush with his horns wedged firmly and diagonally in the hinges of the side panels top and bottom.

With halter now on his nose and round his horns he was persuaded to wriggle up as far as the yoke, got one horn stuck firmly in the mechanism and could not budge him for a full quarter hour. The only way to release him was to cut three inches off the tip of the jammed horn with the wire, this we did as he stood calmly watching through one eye. The instant it cut through he stepped forward and he was duly in the yoke.

He is a Hereford bull that I bought last year and is about three years old, it is his first calves that are dropping now.

We then put a second halter on to try to stop his throwing his head about and proceeded to injected round the base of his horns with Lignocane to freeze the area. As you can imagine he was not too keen on that, and then we checked over the cutting wire and its handles on each end, and the lad helping me flexed his muscles as an athlete would and the tension grew. Wire went round the first horn just up from the flesh, and started the sawing, it gradually sank in out of sight, a little dust or smoke from the heat was soon stopped as we hit first blood. It had the function of lubricating the wire, and the cutting continued.

After around three or four minuets cutting, the horn eventually dropped off, a nice clean cut but we had three spurts of blood, the two smaller ones were dabbed with a hot iron but the main flow the iron would not stem. This was when we fell back onto what the vet did some years ago in the same situation; we plugged it with a match stick.

The second horn we cut the same but the bull was getting a bit annoyed and throwing his head about breaking one halter and the snatch against the wire we broke the end off the wire. I think my mate was glad of a pause and a breather while the end was threaded back on the wire. On again with the blood lubrication helping the cutting, until the second dropped to the ground.

By this time the first match stick had been knocked out and four spurts of blood fountained up, however like a good boy scout I had got two hundred and fifty more matches in me pocket. With a bit of hot iron and by now three matches sticking out of each horn wound the flow was well under control. What blood he did loose would easy fit on a shovel and he had got plenty more to keep him going. Never again will he get his head jammed in the race and crush or in the feeder in the winter, he was released back into the field looking a little dazed and bewildered, and walked off to find the cows.

The following morning the bull had congealed blood all down each side of his head made to look all the worse by the fact that he has or had a white head. Most Hereford cattle have horns that curl gentle forward but this chap his horns went out a good three feet wide, he never used them other than rub his head in a sand hedge bank, and he does not seem to be any worse for ware after his operation.

We endeavour to dehorn the cattle as calves, a lot easier to handle at that age, but when a calf kicks it can certainly whip its legs out fast.

New born calves do try to hide when they have got their belly full of milk

I Remember Father's Cattle

In the mid 1950's vets were recommending worming young stock with a new product called phenothiazine. This was a powder and had to be mixed with water and a pint or so was pour down their throats. (drenched)

I remember father counting,
Cattle each and every day,
He counts and looks at every one,
To see they're all OK,
Now one day he see's one cough,
And then it was another.
If we don't do something quickly,
We'll be in a bit of bother.

So off down he goes to get,
Some wormer in a rush,
And back he comes and reads the label,
Says get them in a crush,
No crush have we, but four strong lads,
We'll get them in a stable,
Mix water and green powder in a bucket,
Put it on the table.

Four long neck bottles we did find,
For dosing all the cattle,
Phenothiozine, it's called,
And keep it stirred or it will settle,
The pop had gone as we made sure;
We loved the fizzy taste,
One pint and half was dose that's needed,
Over dose was waste.

Pint ladle and a funnel now,
Into the bottled it was measured,
Us lads went in among the stock,
As tight as they could be,
The bottles we did pass to one,
Who had ones chin held high,
Uptip the med-sin to back of throat,
Do not look down or ni.

The cow that coughs, coughs both ends,
And chuck it back they try,
It's just a waste as we were told,
But hits you in the eye,
Soon learn to leave it quickly,
As soon as we could shift,
As dosing cattle get there own back,
Now who's being thrift.

We often wondered why we lads,
Had grown so big and strong,
When other lads around us,
Were only lean and long,
Put it down to fresh air,
And read farmers weekly magazine,
But all the time it wasn't,
Twas Phenothiazine.

**The friendly cow all red and white, I love with all my
heart,
She give me cream with all her might, to eat with apple
tart.**
Robert Louis Stevenson (1850-1894)

Chapter 18

Moles

It's spring time again when the moles start digging and pushing up soil in their inimitable way. Nearly always on the best bit of lawn, following in the hedge bottom then branching out under the grass in the most unpredictable directions.

In the fields they work the same pushing soil up into mowing grass which inevitable get into the mown sward to contaminate the silage heap.

A bit later in the season the tunnels get well established and where the ground goes very hard, particularly where cattle funnel towards a gateway compacting the soil, they will have dug a tunnel across that way and now its too hard to dig another.

Father always said this will be like a trunk route where all the moles in that field will pass through at some time or the other, making it the prime place to set your mole traps.

You are able to re-set the trap in the same place until all are caught.

These Little Creatures Burrow

These little creatures burrow,
And dig endlessly all day,
In total darkness all their lives,
Don't have time to play,
Every here and there they push,
Mound of soil up top,
In the most annoying places,
N' nout to make them stop.

Their coat is fine and silky,
And it brushes either way,
Because in tiny tunnels,
Shunt backward with no delay,
In good rich soil finding earth worms,
Catch them unaware,
To feed his busy little body,
With no one will he share.

His feet are as little spades,
To dig a longer tunnel,
And with his back feet shove the soil,
Up a little funnel,
This is when you see soil move,
Pushed up from below,
A mole is what I'm looking for,
Just to say hello.

At one time we had a family of moles working there way
across a low area of meadow ground, running into a
substantial depth of peat. Every now and then we get a
summer flood just after we had got all the silage bales away.
This one particular year we were in the middle of actually
baling with the small conventional baler, and left the baler on
the meadows. Over night there was a substantial down pour,
and the ditches and the brook that they run into are well
weeded up and it impedes the flow. So it did not take much
for the meadow to flood, much to the annoyance of the

moles.

I went to retrieve the baler in about six inches of water, and to my amazement saw a couple of moles swimming for dear life in the wrong direction. Of coarse it was much too dangerous for me to follow them, as the area is dissected by deep drainage channels, the flood levelled the meadows so you could not see where they are.

We have called cattle off those fields in flood from time to time, the older ones seem to sense where to go, but the followers, that year's spring born calves soon find out how to swim, and swim towards the cows.

Our cows have all been born on the place and know not to get in the peaty ditches, learning as calves. Once one has been in the ditch, they never go in again, and remember that all their lives.

The calves can most often get out themselves, being agile and not too heavy, the evidence of which is a black tide mark up to a few inches from the top of the shoulders, although they must be counted twice a day and the ones that are stuck got out immediately.

It makes me wince when you see the firemen have been called out to get a cow out of a peaty ditch, a whole crew of men or perhaps two crews trying to get a fire hose under the belly of the animal. On the odd occasion when I have bought in a cow or in calf heifer, and they got stuck, I take an old cow chain and a length of rope and the fore end loader.

Put the chain round the cow's neck, attach the rope to it under the cows chin, and then fasten to the loader. Lift gently but firmly, and start moving back, the cow's neck looks long at this point, but don't worry it will hold the whole weight of her body.

Once out they stand up in a daze, it gives you time to detach the chain and rope. The whole operation, one man and tractor, ten minutes at tops.   Never lost one using this method, or pulled its neck out, but a horse I am told by the old men of the village would soon get a broken neck.

I was told that before the days of tractors the way was to take the old iron wheeled muck cart, the ones with five foot wooden wheels, back it up to the ditch and remove the horse from the shafts.

Lift the shafts skywards until the rear of the cart is in the grass. Rope or chain round the cow's neck or in them days round the horns, and threaded up over the front of the cart and tied to the shafts. I know there was always more men about back in them days, so about four men were able with a bit of luck pull the shafts down to the ground, and a man on each wheel wheeled the cart forward thus extracting the said cow, (not dead) cow.

When we first had a Fordson tractor and the next four generations of tractors as well, they had no cabs and only later did we have a loader fitted, the removal of a cow from the peat went like this.

Reverse up to the ditch, hitch onto the cow as described before, and feed the rope over the top of one rear tyre and tie it off down the far side. It is important to be dead in line for this, and someone with a hand on the rope easily guides it over the centre of the tread, and gently drive forwards.

The whole reason for this lifting as opposed to dragging, is that a cow dragged will put her from legs out straight in front to pull against the rope and push her front legs under the turf bank and anchor there, that would be a good time to pull her neck out. So lift and pull is the name of the game, this is made a lot easier with the modern four drive loaders.

I think I could give tuition to the likes of the fire men, but as so often happens, their chief know best how to make it into a whole days work for eight or ten men and couple of appliances and maul the animal half to death, creating vet bills on top as well.

Not being critical, its just practical experience, its costly if you get it wrong, and as a farmer, if it hits you in the pocket, it is remembered for ever.

No race can prosper till it learns that there is as much dignity in tilling the fields as writing a poem
Booker T. Washington (1856-1915

Chapter 19

Worms in the garden, and worms in the fields.

Earth Worms

Part of the ecology of the earth and soil that it is made up of is occupied by earth worms. These are only seen when ploughing or digging, this is when you see hundreds of birds following the plough. Worms eat through and draw down compost and dead vegetation into the ground often leaving the familiar worm casts. This gives a natural drainage and aeration to the surface of the land.

Some years ago as a side line to my farming, we had a wormery, breeding and rearing earth worms, for fishermen, and supplying them to gardener's to be put into garden compost bins. It was very interesting in that, you could use the natural instincts of the earth worm, in order to "harvest" them or separate them from their eggs.

Initially we bought five thousand worms as a starter pack, and introduced them fifty at a time into a peat / rotted horse muck mixture in plastic bins or boxes measuring 12 x 18 inches by 12 inches deep (for metric modern folk its, 30 x 45 mm and 30 deep) this was then covered with a bit of old carpet to keep the whole lot moist.

They were stacking boxes as used in offices and store houses, and the worms could be stacked three high on trestle tables up out of the draught and kept at a temperature of no less than 60F. Each week they were checked for moisture to see the compost was not drying out,

And after six weeks the fifty worms had "eaten" the rotted horse muck and the litter had to be renewed.

Each box was tipped out onto a table, any worms exposed soon burrowed deep back into the pile, the litter on the outside of the cone was gradually scraped away driving the worms into the centre.

Repeating this a few times within a few minutes you are left with a pile of just clean worms all trying to get under each other away from light, forgot to say you need a bright light on above the table while doing this job as it makes them move even faster. The piles of fifty worms are put back into their box with new peat and rotted muck and the carpet replaced.

The spent litter on looking carefully is full of eggs, this is put into a box double the size of that they came out of, along with an equal proportion of new peat/muck mixture, a piece of carpet placed on top and keep an eye on the moisture of the boxes over the next month or so.

It's quite exciting to find your fist hatchlings so small you can hardly see them. After a few more weeks the young worms can be tipped out with there own litter into a main muck ruck, or compost heap if that's what you like to call it. This again must be covered with a large carpet, or something similar, and every week taken off and add another layer of rotted muck. You can hose pipe spray on top of the carpet if it's too dry, and the young worms will eat their way up from the compost below up into the muck. After ten or twelve weeks the worms will be approaching adult size, almost ready to breed themselves.

There are a number of ways of catching these worms when they are ready for sale, you can spread a fine mesh over the litter before you spread the next lay of muck, only a very thin layer, and the mesh needs to be big enough for the worms to get through. Then replace the carpet and moisten in the usual way, after a few hours or perhaps the following morning most of the worms are in that top layer above the mesh. Remove the carpet, and rollup the mesh and some litter and nearly all the worms from that area, and tip them onto a table beneath a bright light, they will endeavour to get to the centre of the pile and what bit of litter you have on the table can be gently scraped off then.

For smaller scale harvest you can used a fine garden riddle with a bit of new rotted muck and place it on the surface under the carpet, you get the same results as described above.

If your main rearing bed is outside, the biggest problem will be badgers, rats and moles, they must be excluded, as if they once find your worm population, they will insist on returning every night. The beds can be of sleeper on edge round the sides as in a raised bed for gardening, instead if old carpet nowadays the top can be covered with bubble wrap and secured down round the edges.

Once the fishermen and gardeners know where you are and what you've got they can be packed in fifties in a handful of new peat in small plastic boxes, with air holes in the lid. They can be posted all over the country this way, (so long as you've got your money in your pocket first). The largest consignment was for a months fishing trip to Ireland for two fishermen, who called and picked them up on the way.

To get an idea of what to charge you have only to go to one or two fishing tackle shops and enquire as to what they charges for worms.

The spent worm compost is ideal for selling to gardener and nursery men as it is completely weed free and stone free, and most of it derived from what goes through the horses gut, then through the worms gut.

When starting a new bed use about a foot deep of the old compost/litter as that is where they reside and gradually eat their way up into new rotted muck. Very little or no peat is used once they have establish their own "living" litter; peat is mainly used for the breeding boxes mixed half and half with muck.

Worms in the garden

Worms in the garden
And worms in the fields,
Eat all the rotted vegetation,
Improve all the yields,
Drawn down into the earth,
A worm hole there to leave,
Pushing up the worm casts,
A little pile of soil is heaved.

115

Repeated over a garden,
Or over acres in the grass,
Drawing down the cow pats,
Does it quietly without harass,
Moving in its little way,
Tons and tons of soil,
Millions of them working hard,
Their little bit of toil.

———————————

Those who bring sunshine into the lives of others cannot keep it from themselves.
James M Barrie (1860- 1937)

Chapter 20

Twins, Twins, Twins,

At summer's end it's parted from, its mother needs a rest,
Life of growing, getting fat, for meat, correct you've guessed.

It has been well over twenty years since we had twin calves born on the place, and could easy be ten years before that when we had twin pedigree charolais bulls born. One we kept as our stock bull the other was sold for service, so its two sets of twins in thirty years.

This year so far out of seventeen cows calved; we have had three sets of twins, five bull calves and one heifer calf which I have no doubt will be a freemartin (non-breeder), so our calving ratio is well over the hundred percent.

On the down side we have lost two calves which is quite unusual for us, they calve out in the field, and in both cases the cow failed to rise at the crucial moment and the afterbirth still over the calf's nose it suffocated.

The first cow that had twins was the oldest cow and they had pulled her down over the last few months, until she resembles a "Hat Rack". Her calves were lively and jumping about and she is a good mother but I had doubts about her milk volume to rear two calves. So one calf was put across onto one that had lost hers, after a few days he had well latched on and they had bonded well together. The other cow that had no calf I bought a calf off a neighbour, the calf was keen but the cow was angry, and she had to be put in the crush to make her stand still, and after about a week I felt that she may let it suck out in the field where she would obviously be more relaxed, and sure enough today I saw it suckling.

The two cows looking after twins, we put into a separate field where there is a good depth of grass, if left with the main group very young calves tend to get lost when mother walks off with one and has no inclination to go looking for another. They can stay separate until they are about a month old, then we can merge them back with the main group.

Going back to the Freemartins, when I milked cows we were short of heifer calves one year, so I contacted a calf dealer for him to purchase for me twelve Friesian heifer calves, this he did and over the next week they were delivered and paid for.

At two years old they were put to the bull and being a bit suspicious about them being in calf, I had them P.D.ed , the first one the vet said this one won't breed it's a Freemartin, the second the same and out of the twelve heifer only two were in calf.

Now dairy men usually keep their heifers calves as replacement but if they had a heifer calf twin to a bull it would be shifted and put in the market, knowing it would not breed.

The calf dealer bought the heifer calves at four different markets that week (all over the Midlands), to fill his order to me. I since learned from an old experienced calf dealer how to spot a Freemartin in the calf ring, and look for certain characteristics, its almost as difficult as sexing day old chickens. But all this happened thirty five years ago, and I must have been a "bit wet behind the ears" then.

But you live and learn.

A Calf New Born

It's nice to go into the field,
And find a calf new born,
They come along at any time,
Day or night or early morn,
Pains of birth alert the cow,
Find a nice quiet spot to lay,
Pushing hard till it appears,
It's over in a day.

Within an hour it's licked and polished,
Up and had some milk,
Then off to find a place to hide,
Its coat as smooth as silk,
A bog of nettles, stalky grass,
Or just some rushes in a tuft
Keep its head down have a sleep,
Predators its out bluffed.

With plenty milk and summer sun,
It plays and grows as well,
Mother gets fed up with it,
But knows it's hers by smell,
At summer's end it's parted from,
Its mother needs a rest,
Life of growing, getting fat,
For meat, correct you've guessed.

———————

The leaves fall, the wind blows, and farm and country
slowly changes from summer cottons into its winter wools.
Henry Beston.

Chapter 21

Farming Into Old Age, (Three Score Years and Eleven)

Driving very cautious,
Cannot see what's round the bend,
Reactions slowing up now,
Braking distance I extend,
Reversing on the mirrors,
The distance hard to judge,
Backing up to a big old gate post,
No wonder it wunner budge.
(And that's just the car)

As you may have heard on the national news, Stafford Hospital has come in for a slating, too many "Chiefs" and not enough "Indians", with the staff who do the actual work getting demoralised. However we have had a close inspection of the hospital from "inside", with my closest member of my family, very reluctantly being admitted under a 999 blue light situation. In other words she had no option.

We found the place spotless; I have no doubt that with all this bad publicity over its cleanliness or other wise, its finally making huge efforts to gain back a reputation of being clean. The only complaint from the patient, when she was well enough to know what was going on, was one of the nurses who when inserting a needle in the back of her hand for a drip, seemed to press and push all the harder until she found the vein. (a clear need for retraining)
They all have their names on, and there is a box to register suggestion/complaints such as that, and I would think they will be reading every note with great care to improve there image. My misses is a tough little bird, who will bite her lip and smile, and refuses to complain, as the majority of her care was most excellent.

We never know when any one of use will need the local hospital, but ours now must be one of the cleanest in the country, I heard it said that the staffing levels have got to be brought up be it doctors , nurses, and surgeons.

Getting old is not an option, it creeps up on you, and it's not until you are pulled up sharply by your ---------- that you realise your age.

Farming is now getting way in front of my thinking and knowledge, suddenly you cannot run like you could even last year, and the paper work in the office and all the records and forms to fill in, and the Single Farm Payment, I have someone professional to do that for me. One mistake and you're thrown to the bottom of the pile.

Passed another Mile Stone

I have passed another mile stone,
Each year it is the same,
Birthday's come birthdays go,
The excitement's getting tame,
Not so quick at doing things
And hair it's gone all grey,
After lunch we have a nap,
And bed times half past eight.

Walking's steady, runnings out,
Pace myself a bit,
Now I have a shooting stick,
On which I often sit,
Got to eat lot less now, the
Weight it going up,
I'd be sent to market now,
If I were a fat old tup.

Eye sight not too bad but,
Cannot read without some aid,
Glasses need up dating now,
The eyes they have decayed,
Should have longer arms to read,
Glasses conquer that,
They hit you in the pocket hard,
On the old ones I have sat.

Driving very cautious,
Cannot see what's round the bend,
Reactions slowing up now,
Braking distance I extend,
Reversing on the mirrors,
The distance hard to judge,
Backing up to big old gate post,
No wonder it wunner budge

I thank my lucky stars that I'm
Being looked after very well,
Still here on this old planet,
Writing down my tale to tell,
Recording what I've done in life,
And all the folks we met,
Come hail or rain or sunshine,
But we still get bloody wet.

———————————————

**About the only thing that comes to us without effort is old
age.**
Gloria Pitzer in Readers Digest 1979

Chapter 22

Animals in our Lives part 2

Holly was a slim black cat that was discovered in the old cowsheds as a three quarter grown kitten. I opened the building door one morning and surprised her, she almost ran round the walls like a wall of death rider. Later we put some food in the shed and continued all that week. Eventually she started stepping forward while the food was being put down, then weeks later she came across the yard to the back door.

Holly had been dumped in our yard, and an identical one dumped at the Aston cottages on the same night, no wonder she was as wild and nervous as she was.
Over the twelve years we had her, she was prone to cat flue, and only once took her down to the vets.

The vet picked her out of the old fishing basket by the scruff and put her feet on the table, in the other hand he had his thermometer to put under her tail. I held out her tail, but she did not appreciate the indignity of where the thermometer went.
She sunk all her claws into the vets hand, along with loud wailing and spitting, the vet went through the pain barrier and he asked Matt to lift her claws one paw at a time and hold them off his hand. By this time the examination table was looking like an operating table, (with blood and all vets blood). Eventually the temperature was ascertained and without loosing his grip, she was returned to the fishing basket, it took a good ninety seconds from beginning to end. (Frantic is how you would describe the consultation)
Holly was never taken there again and the appropriate prescription was always prescribed over the phone and collected. Worming was always another difficult act to carry

out, particularly with tablets, they were blown down her throat, thrown down her throat, crushed in the food, dissolved in the milk, all to no avail.

After a few years we came across a liquid wormer that was squirted into the mouth with something like an eye dropper, this stuck in her mouth and always very successful. In her middle age Holly got very dominating over the dogs, as the dogs got older they respected her space, but learning to respect her was very painful. Often one quick swipe would produce a crop of little holes on the dog's nose with a droplet of blood standing up on each claw mark, this they did not forget too often.

William was an Airedale dog belonging to Matt, we bought him as a pup and when he was about six months old, suddenly was sick and off colour in a big way. On close examination, there was what looked like a worm protruding from his rear. On closer examination, and a tug we realised it was a piece of thread, but it pulled so far then stopped with a yelp of pain from William.
Because his condition had deteriorated so rapidly we rushed him off down to the vet to be x-rayed, this told us that there was a needle on the end of that thread. As an inquisitive pup he must have found the thread and started to swallow it and the needle followed it down, until it got to the last few bends in the intestine and got wedge crossways in the bowel. Here it punctured his bowel wall and damaged his anal gland as well. After his op he recovered well but later in his life his anal gland gave him a lot of trouble.
As a full grown pup of ten to twelve months, we started to train him to catch rats, starting with mice under some small bales of straw.
He was very alert and keen, once he knew what to look for, but he had a problem of spitting them out once he had

chewed them. In fact he swallowed them, and then went looking for the next until he came across his first rat, he picked the rat up gently, and the rat bit him on the lip and hung on.

This made him yelp at first then he got serious, then he got mad before the rat let go, there after every rat was keenly sort and quickly dispatched in a savage twist and shake of his head.

William was a very kind dog with people and other dogs, but because of his size, he was a bit intimidating to people who did not know otherwise. Our yard gate was always open, and he never bothered to clear off, but on this one occasion he went across the road to greet a little dog out being walked by its owner.

It was one of those little dogs that had a bow tied on top of its head, and looked ponsy, and William gave it a sniff just in front of its startled owner, and promptly lifted his leg and pee'd all over it.

The saturated little dog was lifted swiftly up by the owner, only to get dog pee all over her best coat as well. We saw what happened from the distance but it all happened so quickly it was over and William back in our yard instantly, but the neighbour never spoke to us again for ages, and she could not get over the disgust at what had happened to her little darling.

It was the same with boots or wellingtons left outside our back door, William could pee in the top of a wellington boot and you would never know, until your foot was well pushed down in and on, and it was not just a dribble he seemed always to be generous with what he left.

It only happened to me only once and thereafter lay down the wellies as soon as taken off. He was not fussy, it happened to the vet who was changing out of his wellies by his car and splash he had got him, and no end of visitors to the house all had to be warned of the danger, shoes boots sandals any footwear that he could find got scent marked, a way I suppose of marking his territory.

Throughout his life William was another dog to appreciate our principle carer's care, although he was trickle fed and wormed regularly all his life, he never got into a porky state. When he wanted to get your attention he would sit in front of you and clack and chatter his teeth and laugh in his way, wagging his one third of a tail, a most happy dog.

After we lost William we had another Airedale called Sophie, she was a show dog breed reject, apparently slightly to big for the show ring and for breeding from.

We bought her at about eighteen months old, not socialised in any way, and never been off a lead in her life, just lived in the kennels. When we got her home and let her loose on the front big lawn, she trotted round picking her front feet up like a hackney horse, almost trotting blind and in a daze. It took weeks of acclimatisation to get her to settle down and be used to being free.

Matt built her a run outside of her kennel, were not too keen on dogs tethered on a chain, so when she was in the run and kennel she relaxed back to what she had been brought up to.

A lot of people got to feel the teeth of Sophie, she was totally unreliable with anyone outside of the immediate family. The vet came to give her a jab, a jab that dogs have to have annually, we called her to us as she was running about the yard, I held her head and one hand tightly round her jaw, and the vet pinched up the skin in the scruff of her neck and the job was done in seconds.

Sophie trotted away in disgust, and took a wide circle round vehicles and tractors then ran up behind the vet at the boot of his car, with a quick sharp nip she got her own back on him and drew blood from his elbow, as if to get revenge on him.

On another occasion she caught a fuel tanker driver as he stepped backwards down from his vehicle, biting him on the back of his leg above the knee. We were very apologetic and took him into the shed and he dropped his trousers to reveal four fang puncture marks right where he sat on in his seat.

He laughed it off at the time, but later we found out he had driven directly back to the depot, and was taken to hospital for a jab against lock jaw.

There were not many people who had not had a narrow escape from her teeth, and it got that she was only let free around the yard , with the yard gate shut, when one of us were working about the yard and buildings.

We were unfortunate to have to have her put down eventually, as she had ventured onto the road and nipped an old ladies arm, her family were very adamant that they would report the incident if we did not have her destroyed. So after a happy home life Sophie never really got socialised to other people, and never dropped the habit of biting people.

While we did still have Sophie we acquired a Jack Russell called Milly she was around a year old, to read her story "Animals in our lives" and of coarse the inevitable odd stray cat turns up, this is the story of one black cat.

We've got a Big Black Stray Cat

We've got a big black stray cat,
With a belly fit to bust,
Thought she's having kittens,
Within days it was a must,
Been that way for five months now,
That's the way she's built,
Curled up in a nest of hay,
Almost like a quilt.

128

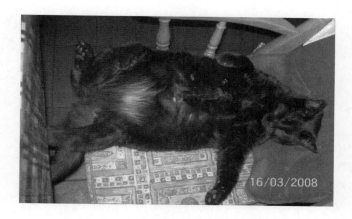

16/03/2008

Very wary when approached,
Must be catching plenty mice,
It was August when we saw her;
She was looking very nice,
Used to us working round her,
Let her sleep and have a rest,
Doing a good job round the farmyard,
Controlling all the pests.

As it got cold found cardboard box,
Keep the draught at bay,
After a week or more we moved the box,
Closer to our way,
Till the box was in the porch,
She spent hours curled up in their,
Fed her a few titbits from a dish,
So easy did she scare?

We put a kennel instead of box,
More comfort for the cat,
Polystyrene in the bottom,
A total insulation matt,
A fabric igloo then insert,

129

For comfort beyond her dreams,
Spent hours and hours asleep in there,
Doing nothing so it seems

A bet was on that this fat cat,
By Christmas in the house,
And sure enough when it got cold,
Into back door forget the mouse,
Did not like door the being shut,
Looked for a quick way out,
So nervous in a new surrounding
Looked to see who's about.

Gradually she gained trust in us,
And found the Rayburn warm,
Made a nest off the floor,
By chimney breast, new cover adorn,
Settled in well for Christmas,
Start of a new routine,
Curled up warm day and night,
A couple of breaks in between.

Lazy comes to mind right now,
As all her food is in a dish,
Only got to stand up,
And it's all there for when she wish,
So now we've got to name her,
This enormous 'two ton' cat,
Samantha what we call her,
But for short it's Sam, (it's short and fat).

———————

Dogs are not our whole life, but they make our lives whole. Roger Caras

Chapter 23

My People Profile

Over the last few years I have been writing about local people, in fact I call it my people profile, only need a few facts and likes and dislikes and what they do in life and how they do it and what they look like doing it.

One well known gentleman in our village has his name spread all over the UK six days a week; he has a haulage company with other depots in Devon and in Scotland. He is a self made man, whose father was a farmer and started by hauling cattle pig and poultry food in sacks from the docks at Liverpool for the local corn merchant on a four ton Morris Commercial drop side lorry, a replica of which he had restored just to remind him of his humble beginning.
So this is how it goes

Stan he was a country lad (Robo)

Stan he was a country lad,
Who took up driving Lorries,
For corn he went to Liverpool,
For him no boundaries,
Starting very early,
Before the M6 was built,
And back again with a full load,
Always at full tilt.

Hard work it was all in sacks,
All handled on and off,
Delivering round lanes to farms,
No time for him to scoff,

Got so busy, bought another,
Set a driver on,
Repeated this so many times,
So busy is this mon.

Still a big tall fit man,
But growing round the girth,
Proud of what he's achieved,
Over all the years since birth,
Globe trotting now and then he goes,
To sample different beers,
Or that is his excuse,
For gut full of dam good cheer.

He's good to his community,
And helps out where he can,
More time he's got to chuck it about,
Has he got a plan,
Looking out where things are needed,
Always ask his advice,
Failure is not a word he knows,
No need to ask him twice.

Stan's he's lost some hair now,
Blown it off with speed,
A natural tan, a ruddy face,
To tan in sun no need,
Has his tinted glasses on,
For without them he can't read,
They help him look around now,
Where he can do good deed.

Stand on almost any motorway bridge anywhere in the

country, and after a few minuets you will see a "Robo" wagon go by.

Another chap who is an accountant lives in the village

Geoff C.

This man he is a countant,
And he works all alone,
This he does from his old house,
That he calls his home,
Converted from a stable yard,
Coach house the lot,
Moved there from the Paddocks,
We thought he'd lost the plot.

He adds up people's money,
To give the chancellor a share,
And what is left he takes cut,
To make a living (bare),
I'm sure he'd have a smile,
When he gives you his bill,
"Never mind you will cope",
If your business caught a chill,

This man if he were in a line up,
Might reach five foot eight,
And eight stone when he's wet through,
Too skinny even for bait,
Slight stoop forward in his stance,
With pouring at his keyboard,
His forehead getting higher,
But by his family he's adored.

When he stands talking,
Fists deep down in his (empty) pocket,
Elbows locked straight,
As if reaching to his elusive wallet,
His ever smiling eyes peep out,
From underneath his lids,
Lids come down to ten past twelve,
Through counting all his quid's.

A caring thoughtful man,
Like the true Brit he is,
Keeps his chin up high,
Even though we take the piz
Over all the world he'd help you ,
Do everything he could,
Even if the council say,
Your house in danger from a flood.

_____

Paul he drives a Fastrac

Paul he drives a Fastrac,
Shooting everywhere,
For to make baled silage,
Never much time to spare,
Does his best to satisfy,
His customers' enemas,
Gets on and gets the job done,
Rolling up the grass.

He will come to mow the fields,
Takes very wide cut,
This to save on fuel,
And fewer turns and passes but,
A bigger tractor to drive it,
Keep it spinning full tilt,
Spread the grass behind,
Just to let it wilt.

Now all rowed up into a swath,
His baler then he hooks,
Picks it up in no time,
N' the number of bales he books,
Often brings a man to follow,
To wrap the bales real quick,
Ten layers of black plastic,
Off the wrapper he flick.

Hay he bales and straw as well,
Keeps him going all day,
Following a combine,
Follow the rows n' not go astray,
For working late into the night,
Tiredness gets a hold,
Hard at work all hours is he,
For his pot of gold.

Recommend this man to come,
Keeps in touch by phone,
Tells you when he'll be there,
For this he is well known,
Knows how long a job will take,
Travelling time as well,
If he has a holdup,
Soon gives you a bell.

A big tall bloke with a smile,
Likes to have a chat,
But not for long work to do,
Never wares a hat,
Prefers you to climb aboard,
Ride round while he works,
That way it breaks up his day,
No one can say he shirks.

Mullee's the bloke, Mullee's the name,
Mullee's the one to call,
Goes everywhere for everyone,
As out of bed he crawls,
Bale the grass, bale the hay,
Bale the straw and all,
"Come and bale me grass right NOW",
Told to ask for PAUL.

Take a rest, a field that has been rested gives a bountiful crop
Ovin (43BC - 17AD)

Chapter 24

Another old Village Character

Old Mrs. Blakmore.1948

She was the last to live in her old cottage,
Thatch had rotted away,
Half-timbered filled in with brick,
And they were built that way,

Churchyard Cottages.

The old thatched half timbered cottage that used to stand not fifty paces west of St Chads Church tower, was occupied by Mrs Blakemore. In my earliest memories her husband was still alive, but retired. Her front wicket was opposite the rickyard gateway of Church Farm.

This ran straight up alongside the high hedge bank of the Church Farm garden, to her front door. The front door was the only door to her house, with a window to the left of it, letting light into the sitting room.

A small window to the right just round the corner let light into the scullery, where there was an old brown sink mounted on two pillars of bricks.

Here the washing was done in her "Dolly tub", and the old "Mangle to squeeze the water out, before hanging it out on the line in the garden. The only other window was above the front door, to the only bedroom she had.

The old oak front door, made heavy by layers of paint, had a door latch that you gripped, and pressed the catch with your thumb, to open.

On the inside it had a large bolt to secure the door; it did not seem to lock when you went out. A new Yale lock was fitted, and it took the old lady some time to get used to it, in fact she walked out to fetch some coal one morning, and it blew too. She had locked herself out, my father who was working across the road, at Church Farm, fetched me from school, to squeeze me through the scullery window, to unlatch the new Yale lock.

On entering the door, you would notice a thick heavy beam, which stretched from the middle of the inglenook, to the left of the front door.

Another equally large beam, which stretched all across the fire place to form the inglenook. Almost the length of this inglenook beam was a mantle piece shelf.

This had a strip of material fastened to the front edge like a pelmet, it was dark red velvet, edged with tassels, but in the dimly lit room, it was in fact very smoky light red.

But it looked very impressive to my young eyes. Other smaller oak beams stretched the other way to carry the floor boards of the bedroom. It had a cast iron open fire place, which had an oven to one side of it, and a chimney crane that swung the kettle over the fire to boil.

In the left far corner, concealed by a door, to keep the draughts out was the stairs that twisted up round a single post directly into the bedroom.

In the bedroom, was a huge chimney breast, constructed of oak frame, filled in with wattle and daub. You certainly would not want to have a chimney fire.

Mrs. Blakemore herself was a wiry and tough old lady, always very busy round the house, keeping it spick and span. Always a very alert and keen to talk to visitors, although she got very deaf in later years, and raised her voice to make sure you heard.

She wore her hair swept back over her ears to a bun at the back, and only wore her hat if she left the front gate. Every house wife of that era wore a pinafore, loop round the neck, and tied round the waist, usually of a floral pattern.

Among her regular jobs outside, was to chop the sticks, ready for fire lighting the next morning. This was OK until she started to loose her sight, then her daughter came every weekend, to chop a weeks supply for her.

Another regular job was to fetch her milk, each evening, from Church Farm, soon after we had started milking. A little bit of pacing up and down, if we were a little late, then we would send her home, [thirty yards] and ten minuets later take it over for her.

At times, if the weather was bad, we popped over and got her coal in, and take her milk. Of course there was the standard outside loo, with the little job of maintenance that her daughter did at weekends; this was standard in all cottages.

I Remember Old Mrs. Blakemore

She was the last to live in her old cottage,
Thatch had rotted away,
Half timbered filled in with brick,
They were built that way,
Wattle and daub up the chimney breast,
Above the inglenook,
Cast iron range and chimney crane,
Hang kettle to boil on hook.

A long shelf across the beam,
Above the fire place,
This was trimmed with a pelmet,
With tassels there to grace,
Rich dark velvet it seemed to me,
Laced with smoke and dust
Ornaments of every size,
For a house that's fit to bust.

Behind the only door she'd got,
A round table made of oak,
Very old by the polished in stains,
Made it look bespoke,
One the shape of her door key,
Where it had been placed for years,
Cast its shadow from the window,
It permanently appears.

Her stairs were in the corner,
Behind a curtain and peg for coats,
Went up steep, almost vertical,
Round a central post,
Into her bedroom by chimney breast,
One rail to stop her fall,
In her only room upstairs it looked,
Just like a hole in the floor.

Had a scullery to the right,
The side of her main room,
Had a brown sink on two brick pillars,
Small window mid the gloom,
Big old mangle to ring the cloths,
Dolly tub n' posher as well,
A greasy old drain to take waste, t
His was how she dwell.

Water was carried from the pump;
Up on the village green,
A couple of buckets a day,
At times some in between,
A tap on the mains came late in life,
Brass one over the sink,
Now getting blind and losing her sight,
Not far go for a drink.

Out at the side a little brick closet,
Under an elder bush,
This was the loo with a wooden seat,
Old news papers used at a push,
Had to be emptied every week,
Deep hole in garden latrine,
That soiled over after a month,
This was an old routine.

When she passed on, a chapter was gone,
House roof fell apart,
It was pulled down to clear the ground,
New house then to start,
All mod cons nothing left out,
Even the drive was paven,
Grass it round, plant some trees,
It's now named "Glenhaven."

2. Green Farm Cottages

The right hand half of the house is the cottage I have described, and the small brick and tile loo is bottom right of the picture. The two cottages were tied cottages, for the farm workers in the village, in this case Green Farm. The thatch started to rot away round the chimney and let rain in, and no concerted effort was made to repair it. The old lady died and the house was pulled down.

It had the very old "ships timbers" as the main frame in an inverted U, the oak was that black and hard, some was cut up years later with a chain saw, it made sparks come off the blade.

Old houses mended, cost little less than new before they're mended.
Colley Cibber (1671 - 1757)

Chapter 25

All Got up Except One Calf

The gut had twisted and the small intestine had gone black, and the large intestine was red and distended with air, maybe the gas has started to blow it up as it had been dead over night.

You may have read my earlier story, twins twins twins, well looking back now I totally regret turning them out on a "home" field, it runs along the back of the village houses and also the village pub. As with all country pubs they are having a bad time, and last night the publican threw a last fling party and later as it went dark brought out his boxes of fireworks. I could hear some of them going off in our house, particularly a firework the spits a banger high in the air every four or five seconds a dozen times, and explodes about forty foot up in the air.

This morning (8th June 2009)I went to look round the stock and went into this "home field", all four cows and six calves were laying down not twenty five yard from the pub, all got up except one calf, and that was lying flat out. It was dead, a huge five week old black Hereford cross bull calf, it was clean, no marks on it, no bite marks, no sense of stress to it at all.

After speaking to the vet about possible poisoning, with yew or some other garden hedges that are evergreen, or the possibility of whether it has eaten lawn mowing's, (I know that will kill horses) we came to the conclusion the best thing was to take it to the hunt kennels and get them to open it up.

It was dually opened up only to find that all the small intestine had gone black, and the large intestine was red and distended with air, maybe the gas has started to blow it up as it had been dead over night. However it looked as though it

143

had got a twisted gut, and the one section was dead, we looked at the stomach contents, it was full of grass, in of the other stomachs was full of milk already looking like a ball of cheese, it had been eating and drinking right up to the point of when it twisted its guts.

It was a 90/100 kg calf, five weeks old, health and growing fast, and it was a twin, in the market it would be in excess of two hundred and fifty pounds. We cannot prove it was the fireworks that triggered it of, but the co incidents was their.

On most of the occasions the publican tells us of any firework display, so we can move stock and ponies away from the adjacent fields, but he let these off on impulse, (or could it be malicious).

We will never know, but I will be very careful not to put very young stock in that field again.

Like I was told from my very early days of farming "where you've got livestock, you've got dead stock".

Thought at the time that it was too good to be true to have three sets of twins in one year, and be well up on my calf/cow ratio, but that's life.

To cherish what remains of the earth and to foster its renewal is our only hope of survival.
Wendell Berry.

Chapter 26

Day Out to the Sea Side (1947)

As kids, one of the ways to get us to go to Sunday school was to put on a trip to a pantomime around Christmas time or a trip to the seaside, usually New Brighton, that's just along the north coast of Wales. This was chosen because it is the nearest coastal destination from where we live.

So every Sunday that we attended Sunday school we had a stamp stuck in a book, and unless we had all the stamps over the six month period, we could not go; the same went for the pantomime.

At the age of five or six or seven nothing was more important than going on a luxurious coach, a twenty nine seater, where the driver sat in the same compartment as the passengers, where we could see how he drove the bus, and watch all the controls he used, watch him change gear, and how the Bedford petrol engine accelerated, how the gear box in third gear had that distinctive whine. We would get off the coach at the halfway mark and marvel at how warm the huge tyres were, and were given time to "water the horses" before climbing aboard again.

At certain points as we neared our destination we were told to see who could see the sea first, then a huge cheer would go up, then out of sight again for a while then cheer again.

It took best part of three hours to make the seventy five miles journey, there was no such thing as motorways back then, and dual carriageways were very few and far between. I remember all the heavy goods vehicles had a

20mph sign on the rear end, and that was their limit when loaded, and often it was these H G V's that hampered the progress of other road users.

.Eventually we all got off the coach with our mothers and headed for the beach, those that had been before knew what the routine was, and promptly stripped off and into swimming trunks and off into the edge of the sea.

Mothers of coarse had come well prepared with a huge bag with towels and sandwiches and pop and all spread out a towel to sit on to watch the kids did not get washed away. However this is a shortened version of how the day usually went.

A Day Out to the Sea Side

As kids we went to Sunday school,
Every week the same,
Had a stamp stuck in a book,
For religion is why we came,
Come the summer they booked a coach,
An outing to the seaside,
Always was New Brighton,
Pent up, a good three hours ride.

Started early from the village,
Pee stop on the way,
Glimpse the sea from way back far,
Us kids we shout hooray,
Every glimpse from way back far,
Loud cheer us kids we clapped,
Couldn't wait to hit the beach,
In that bus we were trapped.

Stripped off behind a towel,
That our Mothers held,
Into trunks and off down the beach,
Into the sea we yelled,

With bucket n' spades, built a castle,
With flag on the top.
Dug a moat all around it,
Filled with buckets of water we slopped.

Then a strong wave came,
Filled it faster than it oughta,
Too much now it over flowed,
Filled it up with sea water,
Build a dam to hold it back,
And faster still we dug,
Now we know the power of the sea,
To hold it back, silly mugs.

Mother spread a towel out,
To have a picnic on the sands,
Sandwiches in door steps,
Large bites we took with gritty hands,
Cake as well she had made,
Then washed it down with Corona pop,
So tiring was that long day out,
Slept all way home without a stop.

———————————

Surprising as it may be, there were no end of the older
generation back then who had never seen the sea, I know my
parents had been in their younger days on a coach trip to the
sea in what they then called a Charabanc, the forerunner to
today's coaches.

It was open sided and had wooden slatted seats the stretch
right across the width of the vehicle and a running board /
step along each side to let people get on and off. It had blow

up tyres and wooden spoke wheels carrying about twenty five passengers, these were sheltered by a full length canopy that covered the driver as well.

In the 1950's father bought a bit bigger car that would accommodate all six of us, plus luggage, and for a few years we all went on holiday together to the sea side. When us oldest two left school, we were left "home alone" so to speak, to cook for our selves and do our regular jobs on the farm.

Each morning mothers regular helper would call for an hour and do our washing up, and upon checking in the pantry she found fly blown bacon, bacon that should have been put in the pantry safe, (safe in this case is a fine wire mesh store cupboard that was designed to keep flies off food but let it be ventilated at the same time, before the refrigerator had been invented). My brother and I had just scraped off the yellow flies eggs and dropped in the fry pan, waste not want not, a good hot frizzle in the pan would soon make it safe to eat.

Mother always looked forward to going on holiday, father was a bit more reluctant, but mother had to admit the she always looked forward even more to getting back again to her own home and her own bed.

The most important trip you may take in life is meeting people halfway.
Henry Boye

Chapter 27

Water Meadows
"Bedworks or floated water meadows"

It was said by the old men that the water should "trot" onto the fields, and "gallop" off.

On our low lying meadows there is still evidence of the very old style of management the "bedworks or floated water meadows", where channels carry water onto the fields from the stream. At the upstream end a sluice was built with simple grooves in the brickwork where balks of timber could be slotted in to hold the stream to a suitable hydrostatic head where by it was diverted along carrier channels around the edge of the meadow to be flooded, some times these would be along the top of formed humps to allow the water to reach the next fields. The levels as you can imagine are very critical, it was said by the old men that the water should "trot" onto the fields, and "gallop" off.

Standing water was not acceptable as it would kill the grass by starving the ground of oxygen, the running water carried nutrients in the silt and oxygen and other trace element that the meadows would otherwise not get. In the winter the flooding kept the frost out of the ground and the grass would start growing a lot earlier than non flooded fields. This would go on for a few weeks until spring when grass growth had started.

The main carriers tapered in there length with smaller carriers branching off towards the centre of the field again tapering off to nothing. Drainage channels were intersected (as with clasped hands) to carry the water back to the stream at the lower end of the system.

It can be seen in places where the carrier ditches were via ducted over some drainage channels and where when the main railway line was built around 1875, brick culverts were built to allow water to continue its route round to meadows up to half a mile of more from where it left the river.

In the village we have a Millennium Walk that follows the Millian Brook down from where the road fords it, to an area of grass, a picnic area, here the brook is fast flowing and stepping stone have been positioned to allow walkers to cross. Lower down where it is in a deep channel there is also a new footbridge.

Between the ford at the up stream end and the foot bridge at the down stream end is a four acre meadow that has a small "bedworks" flooding system which the committee is exploring the possibility of bringing it back into use.

The brickwork cheeks of the old sluice have all but gone and would have to be rebuilt, and the main carrier channel that runs round three sides of the meadow have been filled in, but most of the branch carrier channels are still evident as are the drainage channels and the main drainage channel down the centre of the field.

First job to reinstate it would be to establish the level of water needed to flow into the main carrier, when dammed up at the sluice the water will backup up the stream to the ford, as long as the depth of water in the ford is not affected it would be feasible to carry on with reinstating the channels and the sluice.

This would bring back a very old management tool that had been in use for around two hundred years it got neglected when machinery and tractors took over from the horse and cart, so this system has not been activated or utilised since the 1930's.

The Railway Across The peat bog

It's nice to look at very old maps,
All faded and dog eared,
See what has change over the years,
And what has disappeared,
Most roads and lanes are still the same,
So are most the fields,
Village houses have increased,
Built in corners quite concealed.

Can see where the railway has,
Cut through field and ditch,
Diagonally they run to it,
And a culvert they did pitch,
A hundred and seventy years ago,
They dug a line right through,
With bridges over on a bank,
And some went under too.

Across the peat bog they had dug,
And filled it up with stone,
To this day now the rails sink,
The levels they need to hone,
Most of the work was by hand,
And horse and cart as well,
Men of steel they must have been,
The tales they had to tell.

———————

From the Millian Brook around forty acres would have been flooded from three or maybe four sluices, on each one the water returns to the main flow of the brook.

Another system ran from the river Sow, and that covered getting on for a hundred acres with one of its main carries running under a brick culvert under the main West Coast main railway lines. From a vantage point you are able to see the pattern of the channels that had been established before the railways were cut through the countryside.

You must not know too much or be too precise or scientific about birds and trees and flowers and watercraft; a certain free-margin, and even vagueness – ignorance, credulity – helps your enjoyment of these things.
Walt Whitman (1819 – 1892)

Chapter 28

Our First Massy Harris Combine Drill (1950ish)

As a second tractor father went quite modern and bought the latest Fordson, a Fordson Major E27N, basically it was a "long legged" version if the Standard Fordson, only these had three point linkage and side brakes and taller rear wheels.

Along with it he had a two furrow mounted Ford Ransome plough, and a nine tined cultivator, he had already got a set of trailed Massy discs, and he had corn drill, it was an eleven spout Massy Harris coulter drill. This had been converted from a long pole for two shires horses to pull, to a short one with a clevis to hook behind his tractor. He had done a similar amputation on the pole of his binder.

The corn drill now could be pulled at a fast four miles an hour all day, with just the stops for filling the hopper. Across the back of the drill was a long handle that the man driving the horses could lift and lower the drill spouts, it also put the metering of the grain out of gear at the same time.

Now it was pulled by the tractor a "running board" had to be fitted for a man to ride on the back to operate the handle and check that all the spouts were running. This made it a two man job although they were able to cover a greater acreage than he would with the horses.

He didn't stick with that set up for many more years, as the drill was getting run off its wheels, wheels with wooden fellows and iron spokes, and the coulters badly worn as well.

It was after he had changed his old Standard Fordson for a Diesel Major he bought a new drill, this was a Massy Harris combine drill that he was able to sow the fertilizer at the same time as the corn. This had disc coulters and a trip cord for lifting and lowering the discs, and meant that once again it was a one man job.

On good going this could be pulled at six to eight miles an hour, the new Major had six forward gears and the fifth gear was just right in dry conditions.

The drill still had steel wheels and had thirteen spout/ discs and because of the corrosive fertilizer it had rubber pipes to the coulters. Some of the fertilizer father bought was Humber Fish Muck, as it says it's from the docks at Humberside, this was stinking job and came in powder form. It came in fine mesh hessian sacks of 1cwt. (50kg to you lads) and was unloaded off the delivery lorry, carried on ya back into a shed and stacked, then man handled out again onto a cart to take in the field.

Originally father had a horse drawn fertilizer spreader which had two large wheel at each end of a long box (hopper), in the bottom of the hopper was a row of plates, like dinner plates that turned slowly, with half of the plate inside the hopper and half carried the fertilizer out behind the hopper, this gap had a plough type scraper that could be adjusted to what amount of fertilizer was required.

Then just above the plate at the back were two spinners to each plate, these were on a long full width rod to flick the product out. It was called a "Plate and Flicker" spreader. So this plate and flicker spreader became redundant for the spreading on corn ground, although he had fitted it with a drawbar.

When the Humber Fish muck was put in the combine drill on a dry day it went through very well, but on a foggy autumn days it clogged down the rubber spouts and every now and then they had to be taken off and cleared out, this meant a man had got to ride on the back to make sure all spouts were running.

At a later stage the fertilizer company became aware of this problem with these new types of drills and in time the manufacturers brought out granulate compound fertilizer, which ran more reliably through the drill.

These were sold in plastic bags, when these had been man handled on and off transport a number of times they got pin holes and tares that would let in the damp and go rock hard. Then it became palletised, and later still into half ton bags and then realised they could not get a full load of twenty tons on an artic. When the Humber Fish muck was put in the combine drill on a dry day it went through very well, but on a foggy autumn days it clogged down the rubber spouts and every now and then they had to be taken off and cleared out, this meant a man had got to ride on the back to make sure all spouts were running.

At a later stage the fertilizer company became aware of this problem with these new types of drills and in time the manufacturers brought out granulate compound fertilizer, which ran more reliably through the drill.

These were sold in plastic bags, when these had been man handled on and off transport a number of times they got pin holes and tares that would let in the damp and go rock hard. Then it became palletised, and later still into half ton bags and then realised they could not get a full load of twenty tons on an articulated trailer bed and upped the content to 600kg's.

All my years I have ploughed.

All of my years, I have ploughed the fields,
To grow the crops, produce good yields,
Once was done, with teams of horses,
An acre a day ploughed, with frequent pauses.

The pace was slow, but made no mess,
No skidding or ruts, for them to address,
Seed broadcast by hand, or horse drawn drill,
Harrowed to cover, seed sown with skill.

Always a rotation, few annual weeds,
Do not get a hold, not allowed to set seed,
Thistles in the corn, hoed out with a spud,
Walked through the crop, pull all docks you could.

Cut crop with a binder, three shires to pull,
Followed by the men, stook the sheaves by armful,
Stays in the stook for two church bells,
Carted and stacked, threshed in winter grain to sell.

Seeds of faith are always within us; sometimes it takes a crisis to nourish and encourage their growth.
Susan Taylor

Chapter 29

Numbers Galore

Not many folk still have one of these Farmers Weekly metric converters, I still use mine and had it even before I had a calculator. The numbers game has gone absolutely mad in the last thirty years, (1970- 2000) look at the Cattle Movement Service and all the ear tag numbers, and all the numbers involved in the Single Farm Payments system.

At one time the only number that went on your cow or beast you were selling was the paper auction yard number, and the accountant always wanted to look at your movement book to try and trace what you sold and when, but even that only said cow or calf or sheep and how many on what date and the lot number, and all the fields had names and the lanes and ponds and woods.

Every field has a name and grid and Parish number

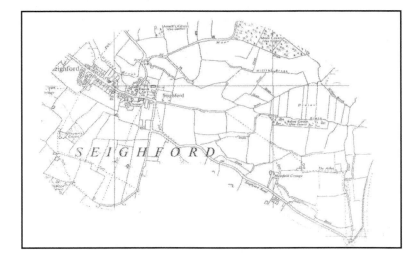

Numbers Galore

Phone numbers and the mobile,
Bank sort codes n' accounts,
Credit card that can be skimmed,
All ya savings trounce,
Car numbers and engine
Numbers and chassis numbers too,
Model numbers part numbers,
colour codes pursue.

House numbers street numbers,
Area post codes an all,
All across the country,
Codes for counties large and small,
Field numbers, map numbers,
Parish number long,
Acres turned to hectares,
If ya know where they belong.

SBI and there's IACS,
Vendor as well,
PI and a Trader numbers,
And Stewardship numbers tell,
There's numbers for everything,
For this that and tuther,
Fill ya head with confusion,
So many thing that got to cover.

Gallons turned to liters,
Pounds and ounces gone to grams,
Miles turned to kilometers
, and foot to millimeter crammed

Therms have turned to Mj's, power
In Hp turned to Watts,
Heat is Btu to lbs, is now
Into Joules per Kilogram it jots.

The moneys gone to Euros,
Bank rate measures that,
Information all in plastic,
And its in your wallet sat,
Converted into bar codes,
So computers read the lot,
Nothing ever private now,
They know all of what you've got.

**Beyond a critical point within a finite space, freedom
diminishes as numbers increase...... The human question
is not how many can possibly survive within the system,
but what kind of existence is possible for those who do
survive.**
Frank Herbert (1920-1986)

Chapter 30

Stafford Vintage Machinery Club
Tractor road run 12 July 2009

This last weekend we went on a vintage tractor road run with the Staffs Vintage Club. It started out at 9.30 am from Ed Weetman's haulage yard near Great Haywood, we headed north and north west up to Fullford via Gayton and Fradswell ending up near the outskirts of the Potteries (Stoke-on-Trent) where we stopped for coffee, this was the first of the three two hour stints that had been planned.

The second stint we followed all the narrow lanes back down the map just east of Stone and on to a Pub at Burston where we all had a sit down pre booked hot roast dinner, as we were a little ahead of our appointed time for lunch.

We stopped at a high vantage point a couple of miles short of the destination to take in the view of the countryside and work out what the distant land marks were that we could see on the distant horizons. Things always look different, when you are looking from someone else's "back yard" so to speak. As the pub had a lot of Sunday lunch time bookings, we had been timed for the second sitting so to speak, and as we descended, on our old tractors, it created quite a lot of interest to those just leaving.

Some of the tractors had to be left on the road side opposite the Pub itself, as the cross over of cars leaving did not happen as groups of people coming (us) and the groups of people leaving stood talking for quite a while.

It must have been an hour and half (or more) stop, and eventually everyone mounted their tractors, and the passengers loaded up on the trailer behind the lead tractor.

My tractor, (Fordson E27N) was the only one that had got to be cranked with the starting handle, so to ensure we all started off together, I cranked up first, then had enough time for it to warm up and switch it over from petrol to vaporising oil, this you can do from the driving seat on some smaller Fergies, but mine it has to be done standing by the side of the tractor.

On our third stint we headed through Sandon, Salt and Hopton, it was here at Hopton that we had our first casualty tractor, an International B250, (MY second tractor my brother in law driving) it had run out of water over heated and stooped, it was soon hooked up behind another similar International and had a tow for the last seven or eight miles back to complete the run.

We continued on through Ingestry, entering Ingestry up a lane next to the Stafford County Show Ground. From there we headed through the village of Great Haywood up farm tracks nearly to Admaston and in a wide arc back into the top end of Hixon.

It was only a short hop then back to the yard from where we had set out.

In all we were told we had covered 36 miles, and we had done it in three two hour stages and must have had two hours for stoppage time, plus a stop while the old B250 was being fixed up with a tow.

There was a little natter and a formal thank you to the organizers of the run before all were loaded up and heading home.

The B250, started, when it had cooled off, and was driven onto its trailer, there was one other tractor that seemed to baulk and its engine stall a couple of time on steep up ward slopes, but it sorted itself out and completed its run under its own power.

We were fortunate enough to only have the threat of drizzle for a few minuets, other than that it was fine weather all day, going against what the forecast said the day before.

Thank you to Tom, who planned and organized the run with help from Jack, also thank you to Chris who organised the refreshment stops. And thank you to all who took part, it all helped make it a memorable tractor road run.

Old tractors large old tractors small.

Old tractors large, old tractors small,
Some go well, some they stall,
Most are older, than their owners,
Some run sweetly, some are groaners.

Worn out tyres, cracked and perished,
Rims all pitted with rust and blemished,
Some come with nose stove in,
Cut it off and chuck it in bin.

New bonnet it will cost the earth,
Sprayed and polished, look like new birth,
New chrome nut for steering wheel,
To finish the tractor, will give you zeal.

Wheel nuts painted or new ones shiny,
New pins and clips, on little chains o'h blimey,
These little touches make the difference,
Get it noticed from a distance.

First thing you're told when first you're out,
"That's not right shade", and gives you doubt,
A clever clogs with brush painted bonnet,
That's my old tractor, he's to covet.

Quite a bit of competition,
Who's got the silliest seat cushion?
Hessian bag on tin pan seat,
Very original, but not so neat.

163

Every one becomes an expert,
Their influence on you exert,
Keep it original they say,
Fibre glass copies keep at bay.

A nice sweet engine, like to hear,
New plugs and leads, and wheel to steer
Throaty roar when it's struck up,
Draw the crowds, when you wind it up.

———————

Happiness lies in the joy of achievement and the thrill of creative effort

Chapter 31

Second report on the Ploughing match

Going back to the clubs ploughing match in early April 2009 here is a second report on the match.

We had a nice sunny day and ideal ploughing conditions and a good turnout of over ninety tractors taking part.

After totalling up the income and expenditure it was found we had £530 to give to charity of which was split between "Headway", and the parish church. Two representatives from Headway came and we presented them with £380 at the monthly meeting, and Rev. Hetherington came to receive £150 for the parish church funds.

This is the Fordson Major E27N that I did the 36 mile road run on last Sunday

We had a Vintage Ploughing Match

We had a vintage ploughing match,
The weather it was fine,
The men had marked it out real well,
The pegs all aligned,
Finger boards at every junction,
Bring the entrants in,
Parked on a patch of turf,
A catering van within.

Puffs and plumes of blue smoke,
As tired old tractors start,
Backings off the trailers steady,
Everyone take part,

Call to see Jack and Margaret,
See what plot you've got,
Then across for a cup of tea,
Ten o'clock ploughing on the dot.

Off to find your numbered peg,
Line up the markers straight,
Clear off any straw or rubbish,
To make your first scrape,
Judges walk round opening splits,
And with a pencil sharp,
Mark the points up on the pad,
Not for us to carp,

Fine and even rough and bent,
Some were all perfection,
Everyone did the best they could,
Up to their satisfaction,

166

Finish crooked finish straight;
Look round all the plots you creep,
Some they falter some they're fine,
Some they're bloody deep.

Oil the plough and load it up,
Then off for a cup of tea,
Gathered round the catering van,
Judges are still busy,
Adding up the points we've gained,
Sorting out the classes,
Seeing who will win the cup,
And see who needs new glasses.

A raffle held and tickets sold,
Money for good cause,
Added to the gate takings,
And sponsors here because,
Going to Headway House,
Headway charity, brain injuries,
Open five days every week,
Support victims and their families,

A donation goes to the village church,
To help the vicar out,
To help the funds for its upkeep,
For this we sometimes shout,
So thank you all for your support,
And made it, a great day,
Pleased to see you here again,
tho it happens to be on SUNDAY.
(The vicars busy day)

Chapter 32

A Hand Can Tell Your Fortune Blog

Hands , they take a lot of rough treatment around the farm, my own father lost two fingers as a lad in the blade of a horse drawn mowing machine, for the full story on that and the poem see "Fathers Fingers".

Another chap who does a bit of my machinery maintenance for me, (the sort of jobs where ball bearings are likely to run all over the yard or where it's difficult to get access to), he has lost quite a number of fingers, another lad who left school at the same time as me he lost three fingers on one hand in the first few months of leaving school, and left him with a little finger and a thumb.

Myself I had a bit of a close shave when I had the skin off the end of my index finger ripped off, about the size of a sixpence, the chunk of skin at that time I thought it would have made a good tap washer, (the old tap washers were always leather) I thought I had lost that finger print for ever.
It's taken a couple of years for it to become tough enough to use as normal but now five years down the line it's still not as thick shinned as the other nine. And yes I do have a finger print again but do not know if it is identical to the one that was torn off.

A Hand Can Tell Your Fortune

A hand can tell your fortune,
And fingers for the prints,
Nails to stop them getting ragged,
Or they look like splints,

To have a scratch or comb ya hair,
Reach in a bag o mints,
Useful for when ya want to eat,
ya shepherd's pie and mince.

Everyone has long arms,
And what is on the end,
To reach around the corner,
In the middle bend,
Fingers at the far end,
For feel on these depend,
To hold them all together,
A hand and palm extend

Hands are thin, hands are fat,
Some are large or small,
Most are there to match the body,
Writing with a scrawl,
Picking up and carrying,
Everything's a bloody maul,
Big hand for goal keepers,
To grip and hold the ball.

Put ya hands together,
And in appreciation clap,
With ya hand closed tight,
On a front door tap,
To congratulate a friend,
On the back you slap,
Sitting in ya armchair,
Hand clasped in ya lap.

You hand in your homework,
But its hand outs that ya like,
Its hands that you steer with,
When out on ya bike,
And its hands that you sing down,
Holding a black old mike
When you look at them together,
They both look alike.

There's a left hand and right hand,
And each has its own side,
When ya want to rest them,
In ya pockets hide,
Writing's only done with one hand,
To the pen applied,
Other holds the paper,
Only there to guide.

Hands you hold each other's,
A helping hand to give,
Sharing out and a caring,
With your hand relive,
A whole lifetime together,
Whole lifetime we live,
Holding hands together,
Each other must not outlive.

I have lost count on how many finger nails went black and
dropped off after being pinched or hit with a hammer, and
talking about finger nails, you often get a ridge across your
nails growing out of the cuticle (if that's the right word) after
some deep emotional shock.

You see it some weeks after calves have been dehorned, they
get a ridge growing out round the top of the hoof, the same

with horse's hooves, it marks the time of stress and you can tell how long ago it happened by how far to the end of the nail or hoof it is.

Stress marks can be seen on cattle with horns, and you can always tell how many calves a cow has had by the number of rings or ridges round the base of the horn.

The first numbering of cattle that father did was with a set of branding irons, not the ones the cowboys used on the hides, but smaller ones to burn the number into the horn or when we started to dehorn the cattle they were branded on the hoof.

Hoof branding was okay, but the hoof grows and the number had to be re-branded in again each year, and not only that you could only read it when the hooves were clean.

So have a good look at ya hands, see all the calluses, the scares, the ragged nails, the lines across the palm of your hand, the lumpy knuckle and crooked thumbs, the hard skin, and appreciate all the work and abuse that they have been used for over the years.

Burnt and scalded, cold and frozen, they are electrocuted on the fencer, and are ripped on the barbed wire, they scratch when you itch and they comb ya hair, they write your cheques, and are put forwards to receive, they lift your pint, and they feed you, what more could you expect from a loyal pair of hands.

We were always told, if we were not getting on with the job at hand to "PULL YOUR FINGER OUT".

It was on my fifth birthday that papa put his hand on my shoulder and said, 'Remember my son, if you ever need a helping hand, you'll find one on the end of your arm'
Sam Levenson. (1911 – 1980)

Chapter 33

Another Mile Stone

*Is this normal, is it what everybody goes through, or am I
wearing out quicker than everyone else.*

Passed another Mile Stone

I have passed another mile stone,
Each year it is the same,
Birthday's come and birthdays go,
The excitement's getting tame,
Not so quick at doing things,
And hair it's gone all grey,
After lunch we have a nap,
And bed times half past eight.

Walking's steady, running's out,
Pace myself a bit,
Now I have a shooting stick,
On which I often sit,
Got to eat lot less now,
The weight it going up,
I'd be sent to market now,
If I were a fat old tup.

Eye sight not too bad but,
Cannot read without some aid,
Glasses need up dating now,
The eyes they have decayed,

Should have longer arms to read,
New glasses conquer that,
They hit you in the pocket hard,
On the old ones I have sat.

Driving very cautious,
Cannot see what's round the bend,
Reactions slowing up now,
Braking distance I extend,
Reversing on the mirrors,
The distance hard to judge,
Backing up to a big old gate post,
No wonder it wunner budge.

I thank my lucky stars that,
I'm being looked after very well,
Still here on this old planet,
Writing down my tale to tell,
Recording what I've done in life,
And all the folks we met,
Come hail or rain or sunshine,
But we still get bloody wet.

Is this normal, is it what everybody goes through, or am I
wearing out quicker than everyone else. On top of what I've'
already mentioned my sense of smell has all but gone, but
thank goodness I can taste my food and imagine the smell
from days when the nose was up to it.

Over the years I have had a few repairs, such as the new
knee's, that was a long drawn out session, it was eighteen
months before I felt the full benefit of them, up to now I have
had ten years pain free, can't expect to run like we did in the

school sports.

It goes back to when seed grain came in one acre bags one and three quarter hundred weight a bag, that's 196lbs, or 88kg in new measurements, now no one's allowed to lift much more than 25kg or 56lbs. You can only imagine carrying more than three of those and a bit more.
When we were threshing wheat for sale, they often sent the hessian sacks, and it was stipulated they had got to be weighed to 75kg one and half cwt. as it was then.

Seed sacks there would be thirty or forty to un load and load up at drilling time, but the wheat for sale it could be anything up to seven or eight hundred sacks, despatched in ten ton loads.
These were bagged off the back of the threshing machine weighed up then wound up on a sack hoist and carried on ya back to the store.
They had to be stacked in rows two high with a gap between rows, to allow the cats to get in and keep the rats controlled, just a few sacks piled together rats would nibble hole in them the same night, Then the wheat had to be re bagged and re weighed and a mess to sweep up as well.
It was usual for us to work in pairs loading onto a wagon with a short stave of wood under the end of the sack, it saved ripping ya finger nails and easier to swing up to that height.
At the mills where the wheat went they had chain hoists and sack trolleys to move them about, it was only on the farms where it was only a few heavy days' work a year on that job that it was all done by man power, and thankfully it was only few more years that combines came in and bulk harvesting was here to stay.

Needless to say all this heavy lifting and carrying was sure to take a toll on the health of the individual, the evidence of which you can see at any gathering of older farmers, bowing legs and far from an upright stance. The old saying "hard work never killed anyone" is right up to a point, as most who have done graft all their working lives, have also eaten well, and very often healthily.

Through all the days of rationing in the forties and fifties, we always had eggs beef pork and bacon, old hen, nowadays called chicken, rabbit, goose, turkey, and always grew potatoes. Every garden in the village, be it farm or cottage always had a sizable patch for vegetables a pig sty and hens. If you were lazy, you did not eat so well.

God gives every bird its food, but he does not throw it into its nest.
J. G. Holland

Chapter 34

Food Miles

Food Miles is such a wide area to cover in a few pages, and is skimmed over to give an overall view of the trends of where were going. This is how far we have got just in my lifetime.

Food Miles

On looking back when I was young,
All those years ago,
The horse and cart were still about,
A lot we didn't know,
Cars and tractors taking over,
Plenty of fuel they sup,
Fuel brought in from overseas,
And local garages set up.

This has snowballed over the years,
Cannot comprehend,
Where all the traffic's going to,
So fast around the bend,
Miles per gallon's going up,
So is car's per mile,
Speed is what's on most people's mind,
Then end up in a pile.

Everything is carried about,
And often back again,
Out to distribution centres,
Finding jobs for men,
Wear and tear on tyres and roads,
Burning up the miles,
Costs all added onto their goods,
Customer pays up and smiles.

At one time, veg came out the ground,
Flour came from the mill,
Chickens walked about the yard,
Pecking happily to get their fill,
A pig was fattened on scraps,
From the house and garden,
Talk food miles, it was food yards,
When things were all on ration.

Only thing that Mother bought,
Was cornflakes in a packet,
Then tins of peaches she would buy,
From other side the planet,
Had these when bottled fruit ran out,
Ate with bread and butter,
Wheat was ground at water mill,
Bread baked next to the butcher.

Packaging's the thing right now,
It's wrapped and wrapped again,
Keep the food clean and fresh,
Or that is what they claim,
Bin through many hands,
And machines to wrap and pack,
Getting older by the minute,
A use-by date on pack will slap.

Where do you put all the waste produced,
Pop it in the bin,
Land fill holes are filling up,
Rotting down n' methane begin,
It all boils down to negligence,
In what we're doing to our earth,
How it's changing for the worse,
All getting bigger round the girth.

177

On looking where it's going to,
Well beyond my years,
Food's way down the list to buy,
As" farmers" get the jeers,
Bring it all in from abroad,
More transport still is needed,
"Look after those who tend our land",
Make sure this warnings heeded.

———————

Wrapped and Wrapped Agen

Food miles are talked about,
From all around the globe,
Fresh is what they say it is,
Had time to gain microbes,
Chilled n travelled round t world,
Tired it must be when,
It hits the shelves, sell by date,
And wrapped agen.

Fresh is when it's local grown,
Few miles up the road,
Picked and dug same morning,
Not long to unload,
To the Farmers market,
A stall all well set out,
Fresh from our own fields today,
That is what we shout.

———————

All this in the name of education, a little more thought should be put into basic living and our ability to feed ourselves in the event of shortages. There must be a few people in power who remember rationing, but I recon those that do were not having to live in real poverty, just shortages, and that's the difference. Not enough emphasis put on self-sufficiency.

Educations What You Want

Educations what you want,
Or that is what I'm told,
Get on in life and see the world,
Seek your pot of gold.
More to life than toil and sweat,
Let others soil their hands,
Let education guide the way,
Nine till five, five days a week demand.

Over the years most folk done this,
For better jobs they travelled,
Men they left the land in droves,
Off into town they pedalled.
With better money they bought a car,
Get about much quicker,
Then travelled even further afield,
Became the city slicker.

Learning without thought is labour lost, thought without learning is perilous
Confucius (551 BC – 479 BC)

Chapter 35

The Village Pump

Just about the last gathering round the village pump before mains water was turned on, this was 1945 .The village pumps and wells were then condemned.

This pump was by the village shop, the other was on the village green by the Church. It was only a few more years that a sewer system and flush toilets were installed then the new council houses were built.

A Well in Every Village

In olden days in every village,
You could find a well,
Middle of all the cottages,
Close where people dwell,
.A big old curly handle,
So shiny from its use,
Pumping all the water,
Cool and clear produce

It had a wooden jacket,
To keep the frost at bay,
Insulate with old sacks,
Sometimes filled with hay,
From half way up the front,
A big lead spout protrude,
To hang the buckets on,
Out which the water spewed.

A sandstone trough beneath,
There to catch what spilt,
Drain back into the well,
That's the way it's built,
A bright green grassy bank,
cept where the people stood,
Worn out by the villagers,
Who carried all they could.

Wells were used for centuries,
Before mains water came,
Then were all condemned,
And filled in for safety blame,
No more well side meetings,
Every morning of the year,
Social gathering of women,
No longer do appear.

As the villagers moved into the new houses so the old half-
timbered thatched houses were demolished, over the years
new private houses filled in the spaces down the quarter mile
Centre of the village.

New Cumbers Council houses in Seighford 1950's

We walked up past the village shop,
On our way to school
Big hedge bank and ditch there was,
Further back a pool
saw them cut the first sod,
Cut up trees burn the brash,
Fenced along the back,
O build ten houses in a rash.

Dug the first foundations,
buv ground built in no time,
Big gang of men there was,
Scaffolding soon to climb,
Next one started same again,
On up to the eves,
Trusses and laths they were next,
Tiles to receive.

When built and nearly ready,
Frontage was dug well back,
Opened up the main road,
kerbed with grass no lack,
New gates and fences,
Numbered one to ten,
Now all ready to move in,
Nearly all were farm men.

People in the village,
They were first on list,
Empty all old cottages,
On this they did insist,

New house and new garden,
Everyone was pleased,
Washing line erected,
Garden path was seized.

On the front lawns were laid
And veg patch up behind,
Competition of, who's first
Produce to table consigned,
All could see what's going on,
No hedge to hide the mess,
Hedge had just planted,
For wind break we must stress.

All mature and tidy now,
Some fifty years have gone,
The old front wickets been replaced,
Although some have non,
Still are numbered one to ten,
Along a wide grass verge,
Only now are these new houses,
Look as though to merge.

Old houses mended, Cost little less than new before they're ended.
Colley Cibber, The *Double Gallant Prologue*

Chapter 36

St Swithin's, It did rain on the 15th July 2009

We have only just passed the fortieth day of St Swithin's, it did rain on the 15th July and true to its legend or saying, it has rained more days than it's been fine. The grass has grown continuously right through the summer and given us very little to groan about, other than the fact that there has not been many "two fine days together" periods that you can attempt to make hay or properly wilted silage/haylage.

St Swithin's day is 15th July, a day on which people watch the weather for tradition says that whatever the weather is like on St Swithin's day, it will continue for the next forty days. I have about a half of my grass mowing area on low lying peat bog, mid-July is very often the best time or the only time when I can get on and drive all over it with the tractors and implements. So far we cut a seven acre patch alongside the brook being what I know is the driest.

It carried the Mower and stood the twice over turning and rowing up with only making muddy wheel marks, the baler, (round baler) came and with his wide tyres carried well but for one small area at one end of the field, the wrapper came along with its small wheels and that seemed to cut in more particularly when he attempted to carry one while wrapping another at the same time, all this on the driest part of the meadows.

Carting the bales meant that the trailer had got to be set along drier edges of the field and the bales carried to it, the problem was then the foot on the drawbar had to have a short length of sleeper to stop it sinking in the peat.

We have had this even in dry seasons, where the foot sinks in, but when starting off with a loaded trailer, the tyre of the trailer sinks into a depression in the turf with the weight, Its like the old timber drug horse teams that were trained to give a heavy snatch to get a heavy load of timber moving (a timber drug horse was never safe to use for farm work as they were in the habit of doing snatch starts and would tip the person off the top of the load).

So the tractor has got to do a snatch start in four wheel drive and in a low enough gear so as not to stall, if it stalled the trailer will drop back into its depression and start to break through the turf, once the turf breaks the wheel, usually only one wheel will drop in up to the trailer chassis, the only way is to unload and start again.

A Verse to St. Swithin's

St Swithin's day it turned out wet,
For forty days its rain,
Each day we watch the forecast,
But alas it's all in vein,
Cloud and drizzle a little sun,
Each day it starts the same,
The next day it turns out fine,
And gives you hope again.

Fifteenth July the decisive day,
And forty more to come,
Whole phase of the moon and more
Before we get the sun,
Big depressions sweeping in,
Low cloud and mist it brings,
Broken cloud and sunny spells,
Muggy warm evenings.

185

The local show the village fete,
A chance they have to take,
It just by luck rain holds off;
Bring folks through the gate,
Just one day a year it is,
And just a few hours that day,
Six whole days since Sunday,
When the vicar's was meant to pray.

Hay makings been put on hold,
And the corn is getting ripe
The grass matured and gone to seed,
But who are we to gripe,
We take what comes from day to day,
Work along as befit,
It's frustrating all the waiting about,
Enough to make ya spit.

———————

Jackets on and shelter for the unpredictable weather for the village fate.

There is a weather-rhyme that is well known throughout the British Isles since Elizabethan times—

St Swithin's day if thou dost rain,
Forty days it will remain
St Swithin's day if it be fair,
For forty days 'twil rain nae mair'

Chapter 37

Two more Animals in our Lives.

With sheep breeding you can bet you will always have some
cade lambs about, depending who has reared then, they can
turn out to be a dam nuisance. We had one, who, as he got
older became positively dangerous.

The Cade Lambs

Years ago had some Cades,
Reared around the garden,
Tame and bold and cheeky,
From us we tried to harden,
But this one tup lamb hard faced,
Nothing put him off,
Would follow close behind,
And charge you from his trough.

Out in the field when he got big,
He'd look and give a baaaa,
He would let you get half way in,
Then start his run from far,
Always from behind at speed,
He'd leap from five foot back,
Hit you with his bony head,
Your hip or thighs he'd whack.

Even if you saw him come,
To waive him off you try,
The charge would be just the same,
The devil he was sly,

Take off your coat, hang it out,
He would be drawn to that,
Like a bullfighter in the ring,
He loved to have a spat.

Word got round, keep out that field,
Cross it if you dare,
Could not see which one he was,
From a distance stare,
Then without warning at full speed,
Too late he's got you marked,
Now it was we must know,
It's his temper we have sparked.

Another pet we had some years ago when our girls were growing up was April the Goat, she had been round the block so to speak when I bought her, and was more worldly wise than the children she was purchased for.

She was always one move in front of them, and found the only way to keep her in the orchard was to tether her.
She would not be led out to the tether, got to be dragged, although there was ample lush grass to eat, so that job always fell to me.
Number one daughter was doing her best to take her out one day soon after we had her and she got her down on hedge bank, and pinned her horns into the hedge bank either side if her thighs and would not let her go.
She would walk back keenly to her shed but defended her food "to the death", and they had to lower the bucket of food and water on the end of a cord over the gate.
Everything centred around food once fed and full they could groom and fuss with her, as long as she was able to lead them

where she wanted to go when out on a lead. We kept her around a year until she became totally dominant over the children.

A Goat Called April

We had a goat called April,
For the children bought,
As a pet to play with,
To feed and water thought,
Give them a little job to do,
When they got home from school,
But she was older than we thought,
Would not be made a fool.

She had long horns up curved,
And use them she knew how,
Defend her rights and show the kids,
To lead would not allow,
Grazed around the garden,
Tethered on a chain,
This so we'd know where she was,
The only way to restrain.

Brought down at tea time,
A feed of corn and hay,
Water in a bucket full,
There must be no delay,
The buckets had to be lowered in,
On the end of a string,
Or she'd power her way out again,
Past you or anything.

Leading she'd pinned Diane down,
Horn each side of her thigh,
Horned dug deep into the turf,
Not move and made her cry,
So April had to go to market,
Next Monday was a must,
Ethnic butchers liked her,
In the pot next week we (I) trust.

The Misses and the girls did not approve of April's demise, but she had to go.

It's better to live one day as a lion, than a hundred years as a lamb
John Gotti

Chapter 38

Oh To Be Plumber Boy (Paul)

In reality he is a farmer, who does all my contract mowing
and baling, but he has trained as a domestic heating engineer.
So here is a good plug for him, he does my boiler servicing as
well.

Paul he has a plumber's job,
As a plumber not mending pipes,
But boilers are what he's trained to do,
All of many types,
Van full of all the tools,
And all the spares he needs,
Inside job keeping warm,
To breakdowns off he speeds.

Of advertising he has no need,
Recommendation grows,
Word has spread far and wide,
Of word alone he glows,
Repair and maintenance,
Cleans and check and test,
Each job he does, each call he has,
He always does his best.

Pull em apart, clean the flues,
Fitting a brand new jet,
Check the vents, and check the draught,
Fuel he always sets,

Then to tests emissions,
Fuel must completely burn,
Seal the front and clean the case,
And test the knobs in turn.

Mullee's the bloke, Mullee's the name,
Paul's the one to call,
Goes everywhere for everyone,
As out of bed he crawls,
Long list of annual calls to make,
Boilers large and small,
Come quick or else we'll freeze to death,
Told to ask for Paul.

Give him a ring, give him a bell,
Give him a chance, he will know,
On O seven nine seven three-
Four nine two, three two O,
He's always cheerful when you call,
Always help you out,
Emergency breakdowns, do all he can,
Tools he's never without.

———————-

**Always bear in mind that your own resolution to succeed
is more important than any one thing**
Abraham Lincoln (1809 – 1865)

Chapter 39

The Home Guard

The railway "lengths men" were a gang of about six men who maintained the railway tracks and fences on their length between half way to Stafford and half way to Norton Bridge based at Great Bridgeford. Father got to know them well as they were also in the home guard.

When father was cutting large field of corn (Wheat) they would hop over the fence for half an hour and help stook the corn, with a gang like that it soon got done. It was the same again when it came to loading the shoffs of corn from the stook. Father always took down plenty of pitch forks in anticipation, and they knew when to be working close by. No money changed hands but he gave them plenty of taters and eggs and in the case of the engine driver he got half a pig.

The Home Guard Contraband (1945 ish)

The railway line it ran through,
Some of father's land,
He got to know the railway men,
Quite a happy band,
They were in the home guard,
And all the farm men too,
They often jumped over the fence,
To load a wagon or two.

For this he gave them taters,
Or anything they hadn't got,
Often at the home guard meetings,
The sergeant got forgot,

194

For this is where it all changed hands,
Just behind his back,
If they ever got found out,
They'd be on the rack.

An engine driver was among them,
He'd got what we want,
He slowed his train by the field,
Tender full of coal he flaunt,
Every morning at nine thirty,
Rolled off big lumps of coal,
Father loaded it on his cart,
This man he did extol.

A coal house full of best steam coal,
Mother to do the cookin,
Big bright fire that roared round flue,
She was so pleased herein,
Only cost a half a pig,
Its contraband you see,
Delivered by dad and Eric in a coffin,
The law could not foresee.

The railway is a four track line that runs from London to Scotland, and every day the "Flying Scotsman" would run through at full steam at 3.45 pm heading north, and back again sometime during the night. It was said that the lines were cleared of other traffic, so as not to impede its progress, quite a number of other express trains followed including some named ones.

.

Local trains were diverted onto the slow lines until they had all passed. For some reason the railwaymen always names the tracks Up Fast, Down Fast, and Up Slow and Down Slow, it was always Up to London, and Down to Scotland. They must have an upside down map.

It was reported by an engine driver that we had had a beast on the line, we went down and a couple of lengths men were sent as well, to clear the carcase off the tracks. On arrival all we found was a half of a yearling's leg and foot, nothing else could be found, we just presumed it must have been hanging on the buffers of an express train when I arrived at Euston Station in London.

To us, the moment 8:17 AM means something- something very important, if it happens to be starting time of our daily train. To our ancestors, such an odd and eccentric instant was without significance – did not even exist. In inventing the locomotive, Watt and Stevenson were part inventors of time.
Aldous Huxley (1894 – 1963)

This book continues in Volume 3

It includes Cattle droving, an encounter I had with a US A10
Tank buster war plane, potato's planting a foot apart (not
twelve inches) folk born in this house (a family with twenty
one children) and many more tales of the farm and village
life.

Printed in Great Britain
by Amazon.co.uk, Ltd.,
Marston Gate.